in GOD we TRUST

STEVE HAM

First printing: April 2010
Second printing: July 2010

ISBN: 978-0-89051-583-9
Library of Congress Number: 2010925433

Cover by Diana Bogardus

Unless otherwise noted, all Scripture is from the New King James Version of the Bible.

Please consider requesting that a copy of this volume be purchased by your local library system.

Printed in the United States of America

Please visit our website for other great titles:
www.masterbooks.net

For information regarding author interviews,
please contact the publicity department at (870) 438-5288.

Master
Books®
A Division of New Leaf Publishing Group
www.masterbooks.net

This book is dedicated to my family —
Trish, Sarah, and David.

May we all truly put our trust in God
for generations to come.

Contents

Foreword

by Ken Ham

Why write another book on biblical authority? Surely hundreds of books on the accuracy and authority of the Bible have been written over the years — and many by renowned scholars.

But this book is different — yes, very different. While it deals with biblical authority, it is written against the background of this "scientific age," one in which many people in the church have succumbed to the secular teachings of our day — particularly in relation to evolution and the age of the earth. It is my contention that many Christians have wittingly or unwittingly adopted these pagan philosophies of our time that have compromised the clear teaching of the Scripture, thus undermining the inerrancy of the Bible . . . and consequentially the authority of the Scriptures.

As a result, the great majority of believers in the Church today can't offer a defense of our faith because they have either not been taught how to defend biblical authority or have compromised with secular views. Both have caused many Christians to lose their way.

We live in an era of history when we see the collapse of the Christian worldview that once permeated the thinking of the Western world. Why has this happened? What is the fundamental, foundational reason for this collapse?

Stephen Ham gets to the heart of the matter in this powerful challenge to God's people as he unravels the Church's basic problem: a lack of belief in biblical authority. This loss has occurred because of a strategic error in approaching and understanding God's Word.

You see, instead of letting God's Word speak for itself and becoming the foundation for a Christian's thinking in every area, believers have been unlocking a door over recent decades that has allowed fallible man to become the authority, not the Bible. We have already seen recent generations of Christians pushing that compromise door even further. In this book, my brother purposes to:

(a) Greatly illuminate the average Christian's thinking in what God Himself teaches us concerning how to understand and use the revealed Word of God.

(b) Expose the true nature of why biblical authority has been undermined — and what needs to be done to have it restored.

(c) Provide insight into God's authority that is so prominently displayed in His very character.

(d) Practically show how God's authority and the authority of His Word impacts Christian living, family, worship, how church is conducted, and how we communicate His good news of salvation.

Many Christians simply do not realize that they don't have the high view of Scripture they think they have. Furthermore, they also do not realize the ground they have given up to the enemy. As a result, they have lost potency in their Christian lives.

This book not only will challenge every Christian concerning their view of the authority of the Scriptures, but will teach them (in detail) about the only approach to God's written Word that a consistent born-again Christian should have.

I praise the Lord that Stephen and I were brought up by a father who never knowingly compromised the Word of God. By instilling in us a high regard for God's infallible Word, our father enabled us to stand unwaveringly in a secularized culture that has invaded and weakened the Church.

I pray this book's fresh approach to biblical authority in this skeptical age will strengthen Christians as they do battle in a spiritual warfare that has already taken a terrible toll on our Western nations, and sadly including the Church.

Ken Ham

President, CEO, Answers in Genesis/Creation Museum

Section One

The Substance of Authority

Chapter 1

Loose Hinges: The Lack of Authority

Agnosticism simply means that a man shall not say he knows or believes that for which he has no grounds for professing to believe.[1] — *Thomas H. Huxley*

Faith indeed tells what the senses do not tell, but not the contrary of what they see. It is above them and not contrary to them.[2] — *Blaise Pascal*

Imagine having a mind so able to reason that by 12 you had already worked out Pythagoras' theory on your own. Imagine by age 16 having published your first paper on mathematics and having it acclaimed as the most valuable and powerful contribution to mathematical science of your time. Imagine still being in your teenage years and having designed an intricate machine that would be essential to the development of modern calculators and computers. If you would desire such a mind, you desire the mind

---

1. www.quotationspage.com/quotes/Thomas_H._Huxley.
2. www.thinkexist.com/quotes/blaise_pascal/3.html.

of one of the greatest philosophers, mathematicians, scientists, and theologians of the 17th century — Blaise Pascal.

Pascal was the son of a chief tax officer, and it was for his father that he designed and built a calculator to help him in the computation of tax returns. From a very early age, through his father's connections, Pascal was exposed to a circle of philosophers known as the Mersenne group. It wasn't long before Pascal was participating in group discussions on his own terms and subsequently became a brilliant mathematical scientist. In 1647, possibly some of his greatest work was completed through his experiments on vacuum. Pascal discovered that pressure applied to a confined liquid is transmitted undiminished through the liquid in all directions (as in the mercury in a barometer). It was also during this time that Pascal invented the syringe. Other achievements included his work in the area of probability, which led to the development of the famous *Pascal's triangle*. Pascal's probability work has been used (among others) in insurance and actuarial calculations.

The year 1654, however, marks the most amazing thing that would happen in Pascal's life. This phenomenon he referred to as the "night of fire." It was the night of his salvation in Jesus Christ. After his death in 1662, Pascal's housekeeper found something sewn into the pocket in his jacket. It was a piece of parchment and a faded piece of paper with Pascal's written account of his own night of conversion. What a night it must have been. Pascal wrote:

> In the year of grace, 1654, on Monday, 23rd of November, Feast of St Clement, Pope and Martyr, and others in the Martyrology. Vigil of St Chrysogonus, Martyr, and others.
>
> From about half past ten in the evening until about half past twelve.
>
> **Fire!**
>
> God of Abraham, God of Isaac, God of Jacob,
> Not of the philosophers and scholars.

Certitude. Certitude. Feeling. Joy. Peace.
God of Jesus Christ.
"Thy God and my God."
Forgetfulness of the world and of everything, except God.
He is to be found only in the ways taught in the Gospel.
Greatness of the Human Soul.

"Righteous Father, the world hath not known Thee,
But I have known Thee."

Joy, joy, joy, tears of joy.
I have separated myself from Him.
"They have forsaken Me, the fountain of living waters."
"My God, wilt Thou leave me?"
Let me not be separated from Him eternally.

"This is eternal life, That they might know Thee, the only
true God, And Jesus Christ, whom Thou hast sent."

Jesus Christ.
Jesus Christ.

I have separated myself from Him:
I have fled from Him,
denied Him,
crucified Him.

Let me never be separated from Him.
We keep hold of Him only by the ways taught in the Gospel.
Renunciation, total and sweet.
Total submission to Jesus Christ and to my director.
Eternally in joy for a day's training on earth.
"I will not forget thy words."
Amen.[3]

---

3. www.theopedia.com/Blaise_Pascal, from Emile Caillet and John C.
Blankenagel, translators, *Great Shorter Works of Pascal* (Philadelphia, PA:
Westminster Press, 1948).

It is said that Pascal was converted on the night that he was reading of Christ's crucifixion. What a night it must have been for him to carry the record of his salvation experience in his pocket for the remaining eight years of his life. From the time of his conversion, Pascal's one priority was Jesus Christ and the study of God's Word. He was greatly influenced by the writings of Augustine and held strongly to the doctrine of salvation by grace (not works) comparable to another theologian of his time, John Calvin. It is also well documented that Pascal believed the Bible to be authoritative. He believed in a real Adam, and a perfect creation ruined only by mankind's sin. There is little doubt in my mind that Pascal had a strong and reasoned faith impacting a fervent heart of worship for his Savior in whose presence he now abides.

Pascal not only left a legacy in relation to his mathematical and scientific contributions but also a legacy of love for our Lord and Savior.

I have taken time to pay the proper respect to the work and life of Pascal before touching upon the one thing that I believe has been a thorn in his legacy for over 300 years. In 1670 Pascal's final work (an unfinished work) on his thoughts (or *Pensees*) was published. This was an apologia for Christianity and was composed of a series of short essays. I am by no means concerned about his whole work, but I do not acquiesce with the part of this work for which Pascal is best remembered. You may have heard of it already: "Pascal's wager."

In a nutshell, Pascal's wager goes something like this: God either exists or He doesn't and the choice is ours. If God does not exist, then we lose very little by believing He does (in fact, we can live enriched lives believing so). If God does exist, we stand to lose an awful lot by believing He doesn't and we stand to gain considerably by believing He does. Therefore it is a good wager to believe He does. Pascal said himself, "I should be much more afraid of being mistaken and then finding out that Christianity is true than of being mistaken in believing it to be true."[4]

4. Ibid.

I wonder if right now as you are reading these words you are agreeing with Pascal. I wonder if you are saying to yourself, Yes, that statement makes sense to me. Why would you disbelieve God on that probability? And while Pascal's statement may have some merit (in relation to the consequences of being wrong about Christ), I would wager that this is not the only reason Pascal came to faith in Jesus Christ.

If I had a mind like Pascal and a heart for the Lord as fervent as his, I wonder if I would appreciate being remembered this way. Imagine being remembered most for making a statement that concedes that to believe in God is to live on the basis of a probability. If this were the basis of our faith, I wonder how we would respond to such issues as tragedy or loneliness. I wonder how we might defend our belief to those whose chief aim is to question the very faith by which we live our lives. To me, Pascal's wager is a loose hinge. In my house, doors open and close only on the strength of the hinges that attach them to their frames. If your hinge is something like Pascal's wager, then I ask you, what else is holding firm the door of your heart of faith? What is your faith hanging on? Is it hanging on a probability? Is it hanging on a family tradition of going to church? Is it hanging on emotion or something that simply makes you feel good about yourself? Is it hanging on a hope that your life might get better because you simply believe? Is it hanging on some dim prospect of taking some sort of control of your life?

Last year two of my closest friends (Terry and Julie) faced a tragedy that many people, including my wife and me, have faced. They lost a child through miscarriage. They had been trying all of their married life for some years to have a child, to finally become pregnant and then lose their baby. To place extra pressure on the situation, at the time of the miscarriage, Terry was overseas with me on a ministry tour with Answers in Genesis. In fact, Terry and I at this time had also split up on tour. Terry was staying in Cincinnati and I was in Los Angeles with my brother Ken while he was doing a television interview. He and Julie were apart, alone, and hurting beyond description. Furthermore, they had only been Christians for around two years, and if anything was going to be a faith-shattering event in their life, here it was. While I was desperately sorry for them in what they were going through, I was also totally confident in the strength of their hinges. I was a witness at their conversion and was now witnessing people who were able to reason on the basis of biblical authority and trust in their Savior with confidence. Terry would tell you that he became a Christian because the evidence confirming the authority of the Bible is overwhelming. Terry and Julie both knew and understood why there is death and suffering in this world, and while that does not magically take away the hurt of loss, it allowed them to hope with confidence in a glorious eternal future. Blind faith has no answers. Blind faith lets you down. Authority matters and it matters a great deal.

Dr. Richard Dawkins and many atheists like him attack the Christian faith. They most often attack at the point of least authority, and usually that means wherever they can find blind faith at work. Pascal's wager is basically a blind faith theory. In his book *The God Delusion*, Richard Dawkins has something to say about Pascal's wager because it is something that Christians often bring up to him as a defense of their belief. If you bring up Pascal's wager to an atheist such as Richard Dawkins, how might he answer your argument?

There is something distinctly odd about the argument, however. Believing is not something you can decide to do as a matter of policy. At least, it is not something I can decide to do as an act of will. I can decide to go to church and I can decide to recite the Nicene Creed, and I can decide to swear on a stack of Bibles that I believe every word inside them. But none of that can make me actually believe it if I don't. Pascal's wager could only ever be an argument for feigning belief in God. And the God that you claim to believe in had better not be of the omniscient kind or he'd see through the deception.

Dr. Dawkins also says:

> We are talking about a bet, remember, and Pascal wasn't claiming that his wager enjoyed anything but very long odds. Would you bet on God's valuing dishonestly faked belief (or even honest belief) over honest skepticism?[5]

Ask yourself a question right now. How are your hinges holding up? How would you answer Dr. Dawkins if he were standing in front of you right now? I can tell you how I would answer: "I agree with you, Dr. Dawkins (in light of Romans 1:20), it's a loose hinge and it's time that Christians repented of the loose hinges we release on society and show that we have a God who truly is the authority and that we can first and foremost stand on His Word unconditionally. In addition, we have a world of evidence that confirms the history in His Word and the confirmation of the Bible's reliability is overwhelmingly clear. This is a discussion I would most passionately love to pursue. Furthermore, I have found the hinges on the doors of evolutionary faith to be very loose indeed."

At this point it is possible I have already lost some readers. First, how dare we agree with Richard Dawkins on anything, and second, we all have different types of faith and some of us just love Jesus because we do. Some of you may also rightly say that regardless of reason, it is Christ alone who saves. But to say that we do not require a reason for our faith is to say that 1 Peter 3:15 does not apply to you. Peter says very clearly in this verse: "But sanctify the Lord God in your hearts, and always be ready to give a defense to everyone who asks you a reason for the hope that is in you, with meekness and fear." The question is, are you prepared to say that this Scripture does not apply to you? If not, do you have the reason and can you answer the questions this world throws at you? The truth is that we are not going to be able to answer every single question on the spot, but that also means the training never ends.

---

5. Richard Dawkins, *The God Delusion* (London: Transworld Publishers, 2006), p. 130–131.

I believe that God would want any one of us to be able to respond with real answers to Dr. Dawkins or any of his atheist colleagues — not to win a debate or to put them in their place, but so that we might remain firm in the Lord and defend His glory, and so that He might open their hearts to salvation through His marvelous authority. A great coach once said that in training, his team's physical exertion is tougher than what they will experience on the actual game day, so they can know with confidence they are truly fit for it. I believe in relation to 1 Peter 3:15 we should be applying the same tactic for this world. Every Christian should be training to answer our toughest critic so that we can witness to our neighbors, friends, colleagues, and families with confidence. We should remember at the same time that this verse says to answer with meekness and fear, and this, too, should be part of the training.

Before we close this first chapter, I think it would be a good idea to test ourselves. How would it go if we were challenged by this world in relation to our reasons for believing in Christ? The questions might take you by surprise, but they are all legitimate questions being asked in our culture, and they all have strong, authoritative answers if you are prepared to do the training. Here is a quick test list for starters:

Who created God?

How can the Bible be credible about origins when evolutionary science shows otherwise?

How can there be a loving God with death and suffering in the world?

How could all the animals fit on that ark?

How could a virgin give birth?

If we only come from one man and one woman, where did all the races come from?

What if Jesus was only wounded when He was put in the tomb?

What if someone stole His body from the tomb?

How come there are no human fossils found with dinosaurs?
What about the da Vinci Code?
How can you know the books in the Bible are the right
ones?
Why can't other religions lead to God?

Well, this is a short list compared to the many more questions being asked in the world today. If you have trouble answering any of the questions above with accuracy and honoring biblical authority, then you have some training to do. We all continue to have some training to do to strengthen our hinges. Regardless of answering the world's questions, who among us can hope to have a true relationship with God on the basis of a wager, blind faith, or a false promise? It's not just about defending the faith or even simply about winning the lost, but it's also about an intimately relational worship of the God we can truly call Father.

Throughout the remaining chapters of this book we are going to journey together in considering if this even matters. We are going to look at some of the consequences of rejecting the authority of Scripture and what authority really does mean. We are going to see how a true understanding of biblical authority can be applied to our Christian walk and how understanding God's authority can have real relational impact between God and us and also with others. Hopefully, we will also see the impact that an acceptance of God's authority can have in how we deliver His good news of truth to a lost world.

It is my prayer that this book might open for you a new world in His Word. I pray that you may also come to the understanding that in relation to your faith in God and in living a life of true worship, authority does matter.

Chapter 2

Hard to Believe: The Need for Authority

They proclaim our madness to consist in this, that we give to a crucified man a place equal to the unchangeable eternal God.[1] — *Justin, A.D. 152*

It is often an interesting discussion. I will be talking with someone about God or heaven or some other spiritual matter and then they will tell me their view. It will often start with the words "I believe." I believe all good people go to heaven. I believe Buddhists have a beautiful faith. I believe there is nothing when we die. I believe. . . .

Actually, I recently had one of these discussions with a friend who told me she couldn't believe in anything where the head or god was referred to as a male. She told me this was her reason for not accepting Christianity. In other words, she was telling me that she believed in anything other than a masculine identity in godhood.

I always have the same response to the "I believe" statements, and it goes something like this: "Please tell me, on what basis do

---

1. www.biblebb.com/files/MAC/SC03-1003.htm.

you come to such a conclusion?" I am really asking them to describe the authority by which they are making the statement. By whose authority can people say where they are going when they die? Most will say it is by their own authority, but others will identify it as coming from someone else. It might be a great philosopher or cult figure, or maybe even science or perhaps some mystical experience. The problem is that sometimes even conservative evangelical Christians listen to people's ideas and think that they sound crazy, but never consider that these same people may actually think that the gospel sounds crazy. I wonder if we ever dare to think how bizarre the gospel sounds to the people we are talking to. I wonder if we could give a credible explanation for the authoritative base for our faith in this gospel.

A couple of years ago I was reading a book from one of my favorite authors, John MacArthur Jr., called *Hard to Believe*. In his book, Dr. MacArthur gives assent to the truth of the gospel and how it is so foreign to the wisdom of this world. He discusses how many Christian leaders have sadly watered down or even changed the gospel message in order to make it more popular or "believable" to a modern, consumer-centric world.

Before we look at this gospel that people find so hard to believe, it is important to define God's gospel message. In so many pulpits today we are hearing a gospel apart from the one described in the Bible. The gospel (or good news) is that Jesus Christ, Son of God, came into this world to save us from the consequence of our own rebelliousness against God. He took the full brunt of God's eternal wrath for our sin by dying on a Cross and taking our sin on His own shoulders. He rose in victory over death three days later and resides as the conquering King of this world. It is His grace alone that saves us through faith in Jesus Christ alone. We all wallow in the depravity of sin, and every human being needs salvation, and only through Christ and His atoning sacrifice is it available. The gospel is not about life-satisfaction or easy believe-ism. It is not about what we can get out of God, or what we can get out of life. The gospel is the deepest, grandest news that requires every human, in humility, to recognize first the wretchedness of his own life and the need for God's mercy. It is in these prerequisites that the gospel gives every believer the greatest overwhelming relief. Without acceptance of the gospel, every non-believer is left under the eternal judgment of an everlasting God. We all have one life on earth to live, and our true acceptance of Christ and His gospel will determine where we spend eternity: in heaven under God's eternal and glorious grace or in hell under His awesome and everlasting judgment.

Think about it. Go tell your friends at work this gospel and consider the reaction you will receive. *Hello, friend. This is what you must believe. . . .* Not so easily accepted, is it? You better have it on good authority that this is true because a lot of people not only dislike this message but think you are deranged. Churches that don't preach this true gospel message are usually growing in enormous numbers and cultural popularity. It becomes about the music, the experience, the humanitarian efforts, or the "victory" in life, but never about the depravity of our human condition and our only hope of salvation. So what is it about the gospel that makes it so hard to believe? What makes it the type of news that would have to come from not only good authority but also the highest possible authority? We could mention many aspects of the gospel that are hard to believe, but let's consider a select few to get the idea.

SIN

Who wants to be told that they have something wrong with them? More than that, who wants to be told that they are essentially evil? Evil is a strong word, but the truth is that sin is evil and we are all full of it. The Bible tells us that God sees the evil within us. "The LORD saw that the wickedness of man was great in the earth, and that every intent of the thoughts of his heart was only evil continually" (Gen. 6:5). It is after this that God flooded the world and spared one family. He then looked at the family He had saved and again saw the heart of mankind. "I will never again curse the ground for man's sake, although the imagination of man's heart is evil from his youth" (Gen. 8:21). The Bible clearly states that everyone is in the same category. We are all sinners. "For all have sinned and fall short of the glory of God" (Rom. 3:23). Not only this, but the Bible says that we were actually born this way. "Behold, I was brought forth in iniquity, and in sin my mother conceived me" (Ps. 51:5).

I don't know about you but I don't know too many people who are willing to say the words, "I am evil" or even, " I am bad," and fewer that are willing to admit it started at fertilization.

In his sermons on Isaiah 1, Dr. Martyn Lloyd-Jones wrote about mankind's refusal to accept sin.

> According to the Bible, sin is not just some slight defect, some negative phase in our evolutionary progress. That is what non-Christians believe. They deny that sin is positive, or that human beings are bad; it is just that they are not as good as they ought to be. But the whole point here in Isaiah is that men and women are positively evil in the sense that they are being controlled and mastered by this terrible power. Furthermore, the prophet says that this is something that is true of everybody — "From the sole of the foot even unto the head there is no soundness in it."[2]

It's not popular but it is the biblical description of sin. Surely if we remove this message from the gospel it will make it much easier to believe and require less authoritative credibility. But then again, it won't be the gospel.

God Incarnate

> But we see Jesus, who was made a little lower than the angels, for the suffering of death crowned with glory and honor, that He, by the grace of God, might taste death for everyone (Heb. 2:9).

---

2. D. Martyn Lloyd-Jones, *God's Way, Not Ours* (Great Britain: Banner of Truth Trust, 1998), p. 58–59.

Not long after its opening, I was sitting in the planetarium of the Answers in Genesis Creation Museum looking at the marvel of God's universe. To consider the number of galaxies, let alone stars and planets within them, is just too much for one mind to conceive. To consider in all of this the wonderful uniqueness of planet Earth as this tiny, inconspicuous speck in the splendor and vastness of the universe made me just want to drop to my knees in the presence of an awesome and powerful God.

We believe that this God humbled Himself, was born of a virgin, and walked among us as a human being. This is either the most outstanding news of humility and love that cannot even be expressed or it's just plain crazy. The God of all as a human child? The God of all limiting Himself in human capacity? Are you kidding?

To those of us convinced of the authority of Scripture, we hold to the most overwhelming concept that we can thank God for every minute of the day. For others, it must just be nonsense.

In discussing all the amazing claims of Christianity in his book *Knowing God*, J.I. Packer makes the following comment about the incarnation:

> The really staggering Christian Claim is that Jesus of Nazareth was God made man — that the second person of the Godhead became the "second man" determining human destiny, the second representative head of the race, and that He took humanity without loss of deity, so that Jesus of Nazareth was as truly and fully divine as He was human. Here are two mysteries for the price of one.[3]

THE CROSS

For the message of the cross is foolishness to those who are perishing, but to us who are being saved it is the power of God (1 Cor. 1:18).

---

3. J.I. Packer, *Knowing God* (Downers Grove, IL: Intervarsity Press, 1973) p. 53.

To accept the Cross, it is necessary to accept that Christ suffered the punishment set apart for the perpetrators of the most repulsive crimes. The Romans never crucified their own. Crucifixion was given only to the most subordinate members of society, including slaves and those whom Rome had conquered. In most instances this method of punishment involved floggings and beatings and signs of utter contempt.

To accept God's way of salvation is to accept that He submitted Himself as a common criminal from a conquered people. It is to accept that He was beaten and whipped and mocked. The Jews could not believe this of their Messiah, and Gentiles found the death of a Savior by crucifixion to be unthinkable.

In his letter to the Romans, Paul considers in amazement that which Christ did on the Cross. "For scarcely for a righteous man will one die, yet perhaps for a good man someone would even dare to die. But God demonstrates His own love toward us, in that while we were still sinners, Christ died for us" (Rom. 5:7–8).

Christ's death on the Cross was contrary to all normal human reason. We would not die for those who are our traitors, but only for those whose love has been proven. We might consider dying for the most noble of causes, but to place ourselves in the way of the most despised death on behalf of those who would betray us is a completely foreign concept. At least this is the way it is for those who cannot accept the authority of the Word of God. For those who can, it is the most wonderful truth, the most relieving wonder, and the most soul-satisfying tragedy ever to have occurred in this world. Reason or not, the acceptance of Christ and His crucifixion has no equal to its importance in life. Furthermore, the authority that brings us this message must surely have no equal, or this message is of no consequence at all.

Self-Denial and Repentance

Success is everything in this society. Do you have a good house, a good-paying job, great material possessions, a strong retirement plan, and more? Is your life fulfilling and do you feel successful? Do you have good self-esteem? But this is not the gospel message. The gospel message is about denying oneself and taking Christ. It is about accepting ourselves as reprobates to accept a Savior.

In Jesus' own words, "If anyone desires to come after Me, let him deny himself, and take up his cross, and follow Me. For whoever desires to save his life will lose it, but whoever loses his life for My sake will find it" (Matt. 16:24–25). Churches that don't preach this true gospel message are often culturally popular. The depravity of our human condition and our only hope of salvation has to be the most important issue.

I was recently listening to our local Christian radio station while driving in Brisbane. A commercial came on promoting an event from an evangelical church. The pastor announcing the conference invited men to come to his church to listen to a gospel that is not a negative gospel but an empowering gospel. "We don't preach a down gospel. We don't preach a negative gospel. We preach life," was his plea. As I was driving I tried to determine what that really meant. Were we being told that if we took people to this event they wouldn't be confronted by the offense of the gospel telling them they were sinners who needed to repent? Could we be comfortable that our guests would be told they could be recipients of a great life in Jesus Christ without having to worry about any negativity? Today's gospel is subtly transforming before our eyes into a gospel that is about success, not self-denial. But the gospel of the Bible is about denying ourselves to put on Christ, and it comes at great cost — His life and ours.

John MacArthur puts it this way:

> So who is right? Is the message of Christianity self-fulfillment or self-denial? It can't be both. If it is just a matter of opinion, I'll do my thing and you do yours, and we'll both cruise contentedly along in separate directions. But Christianity, the genuine gospel of Jesus Christ, is not

a matter of opinion. It is a matter of truth. What you or I want, or anybody else wants, makes no difference whatsoever. It is what it is — by God's sovereign will.[4]

John MacArthur is saying that God is the authority when it comes to salvation, and if you don't like the idea of self-denial it really is immaterial. If you don't like the idea of turning from a sinful life to follow Christ, how can you then follow Christ at all? If God is not the authority, who could possibly deny selfish ambition and in humility accept His lordship? An acceptance of the gospel itself is, and has to be, an acceptance of authority — God's authority and Christ's authority.

NARROWNESS

In our post-modern thinking culture, there is no opportunity to tell people they are wrong and that there is only one truth. Truth in this world is what you believe it is and it's not about being right or wrong. It's about feeling that you are doing what is right for you. Absolute truth is a foreign concept in the modern world, and to stand on absolute truth is to stand in arrogance and to be a dogmatic fundamentalist.

How do you tell your friends that what they believe is wrong? Christ tells us there is only one way for salvation. The only way to the Father is through the Son. In Acts 4:12 we read this about Jesus of Nazareth: "Nor is there salvation in any other, for there is no other name under heaven given among men by which we must be saved."

We can believe whatever we want, and we can believe with all sincerity, but we can also be sincerely wrong. If we are going to live and preach an authentic gospel, we are going to be unpopular. We are going to be narrow-minded in the eyes of this world. But imagine if, with fear and humility, we can explain and defend that narrow message. Imagine if we can show clearly that this narrow message comes with great and credible authority.

4. John MacArthur, *Hard to Believe* (Nashville, TN: Nelson Books, 2004), p. 5.

The gospel of Jesus Christ is the central message of every Christian. We believe (rightly so) that it is the most important message this world can ever know. If we believe this, then we should also recognize that we need to share this message, showing clearly that it comes from God. The authority of this message truly has no equal, but when we are asked to explain that authority, we start to become unstuck. Some claim "experience" as the reason to believe. Some claim other things such as family heritage or a fulfilling life, or some might even claim "probability" such as Pascal's wager. But are these things really going to help people understand and reason in relation to what we have clearly shown to be hard to believe? Are we really going to be able to defend the gospel on the basis of our feelings or experience? Are our friends really going to accept that the incarnation of Christ makes sense because one can feel and experience the love of Christ? Is this really what Peter means when he asks us to defend and have reason for what we believe? Paul says in Romans 12:2: "Be transformed by the renewing of your mind, that you may prove what is that good and acceptable and perfect will of God."

We started this chapter considering that people have different "beliefs" about God (or no god), as well as life and what happens to us when we die. We all base these beliefs on a certain authority. Some may base their beliefs on science, others on a feeling, others from a teacher, philosopher, or religious leader. When it comes to belief or unbelief about these things, and especially about Christ's gospel (a message that is hard to believe), we should first consider what is not an appropriate authority on which to base our opinions. We'll do that in the next chapter.

Chapter 3

Counterfeit: False Authority

I did it my way. — *Frank Sinatra*

There is one thing my children hate — a long drive anywhere with me. At some stage I am going to bring out the old favorite, put it in the CD player, and start singing away: "The best is yet to come," "Would you like to swing on a star," "New York New York," "Fly me to the moon," and the list goes on. I suppose it is that big brass backing with the impeccable timing and clear vocal phrasing that portrays the brilliance only Frank could bring. Yet I could never bring myself to sing "I did it my way" with him. It's like saying that my life is lived on the basis of my own authority. I answer to nobody, and if you don't like it, go whistle. If there is a God, it's not my problem because "I did it my way." I answer to me. Frank Sinatra may or may not have thought about the words of that song more than simply thinking he was putting his stamp on the world. And in a way, he did. But in a way he was also giving his theory on life; his opinion about what was most important in life, to do it your own way, to be your own authority. And to do it your own way isn't just saying that you should have your own opinions. It is saying that you should be your own authority.

There is a big difference between words like "opinion" and "theory" compared to "authority."

Authority is a towering principle that claims an absolute. Linked to the word authority, we have words like *author, authorize, authoritative,* and *authentic.* All of these words come with the implication of both initiative and finality. An author creates or initiates that which people read or view. When this happens, it is the author who is the authority of his own work. When we authorize something we give it approval, and that requires the ability to have the final say. When we do or say something authoritatively, it is from the perspective of being absolutely convinced of the existence of a credible source of power to do so. You can't counterfeit authority.

Is there such a thing as an absolute authority? Is there one authority that overrides all other claims of authority, dominating mankind in all matters? Certainly, if so, this would be God.

Especially when it comes to the consideration of God, eternity, and spiritual matters in general, the question arises: Who is the authority? Who claims the authentic truth? And what is the credibility of these claims?

I don't know about you, but I have had many people tell me that they cannot accept God (especially the Christian God) based on their own claims of authority, such as, "Science has proven the Bible to be contradictory," "I can't accept such a thing as a good God when I have suffered so much pain in this life," and "We have enough power in our own mind to reason without embracing religion." Others in this world have come under oppression from considering God or the Christian faith on the basis of state or government dictates, or through the consequences of rejecting cultural beliefs or traditions. Are these authorities so high that they contradict the claims of Christianity that there is only one God and one way of salvation? This includes human reason/philosophy, science, experience, state/government, and culture/tradition. In relation to God and salvation, either these avowed authorities show Christianity to be little more than capricious fanaticism or they are counterfeit.

Let's now have a quick overview of these claimed authorities and consider their authenticity.

HUMAN REASON / PHILOSOPHY

This world has seen many great philosophers — the people we have called great human thinkers of our times. You will be familiar with such names as Socrates, Plato, Aristotle, Voltaire, Hegel, and the list goes on. Some philosophers have proven to have great ideas that have helped mankind in magnificent ways. There have been men who have contributed greatly to subjects such as mathematics, physics, and even politics. Yet it stands to reason that human reason is limited. Unless there is a human that can prove to be omniscient (all knowing), we have not one philosopher with ultimate authority.

Bertrand Russell, known for his works around the time of World War II, was convinced that human philosophy could never obtain certainty:

> It seems to me that philosophical investigation, as far as I have experience of it, starts from that curious and unsatisfactory state of mind in which one feels complete certainty without being able to say what one is certain of. The process that results from prolonged attention is just like that of watching an object approaching through a thick fog.[1]

If you read any of Bertrand Russell's writings you will soon learn that he was opposed to the thought of "deity" and particularly in relation to a Judeo/Christian deity. He lived by his own philosophical views about the world. At the same time, he

---

1. Jeremy Stangroom and James Garvey, *The Great Philosophers*, Bertrand Russell (London: Arcturus Publishing, 2006), p. 131.

acknowledged that philosophy is a process described as a changing dark haze providing no sense of certainty even if one feels it. The contradiction in this statement is clear. Bertrand Russell was certain there is no God, but based on his own definition of philosophy he could not authoritatively say so.

Claimed by many in the world to be the founding fathers of philosophical thinking were the likes of Socrates, Plato, and Aristotle. Plato, a student of Socrates, formed an analysis that "If something is truly known, it is known forever, it cannot turn out to be false tomorrow."[2] Plato's thinking was that logic is a constant. A triangle will always have three sides, one plus one will always equal two, etc. We can read this and all agree that it is indeed fact that the laws of logic are constant. Something cannot be true and false at the same time. Does this make Plato an authority? No. Plato has clearly shown that he can only reason *within* the realms of logic. This clearly shows that Plato was not the originator or initiator of logic, but was caught within the realms of logic. There is clearly a higher authority. In addition to this, Plato's work on *forms* reasoned that there must be an originator for the forms. Beauty must come from beauty, and the form of man must also be a man (or come from manhood).

Plato's work, while fascinating, has only proven that we as human beings are limited within the realms of the laws of logic and reason, which were not initiated by us, and we are limited in understanding the origins of form. Unless one can actually be the originator of form and laws, one cannot claim authority.

When it comes to origins or consideration of God (and His gospel), human reason/philosophy is limited, and it is these limitations that disprove any authoritative claims.

Science

Science is the systematic study of some aspect of the physical world (using our five senses) in order to gain a true understanding of the world. There are two types of science:

---

2. Ibid., Plato, p. 14.

1. Operational Science

Operational science is a systematic approach to understanding that uses observable, testable, repeatable, and falsifiable experimentation to understand how nature commonly behaves.

Through operational science we have sent men to the moon and invented marvels of technology such as wireless Internet, or my son's favorite — Nintendo Wii. It is also operational science that has helped us find treatment and cures for diseases such as leprosy, and it's the science we are using to search for cures for cancer.

Christians have often been wrongly accused of being in opposition to science, but history proves that many men claiming Jesus Christ as their Savior have made major contributions to our world using operational science in areas such as health, technology, environmental conservation, navigation, etc.

As discussed previously, we are all bound by the laws of logic when it comes to reason, and this includes scientific reason. No single human being can reason either philosophically or scientifically outside the laws of logic. Built on the laws of logic are the laws of mathematics, the laws of physics, the laws of chemistry, etc. No scientist has ever been the initiator of logic where the only one true absolute authority can be found.

2. Historical (Origins) Science

Historical science is an interpretation of evidence found in the present that was left by past event(s) to reconstruct the historical event(s). An example of historical science would be such a thing as determining how the Grand Canyon was formed, or how the eye came into existence, or how this world came into being.

In the sense of historical science, we use operational science techniques to confirm or deny our theories or hypotheses of the past. Historical science relies on a presupposition (our assumptions or starting points). Both evolutionists and creationists have an explanation of the past that is historical science. They look at the same evidence but come up with different interpretations (reconstructions) of the past. The difference comes from their starting hypothesis or presuppositions.

In this way, science can confirm or even falsify whether the evidence fits with our presuppositions about an historical event, but it cannot itself be the authority. Many people have rejected Christ in the name of science and particularly in the name of evolutionary science. The great conquest of evolutionary scientists (and particularly atheists) has been to convince many people that the evidence itself (such as fossils) is old and belongs to evolution and therefore contradicts biblical authority. All evidence, however, exists in the present, and none of it has a date stamp on it telling us exactly how old it is or how it died and exactly how it happened. The problem for people rejecting the authority of Scripture on the basis of "evolutionary evidence" is, in fact, their definition and understanding of the nature of evidence. We will consider more of this in later chapters.

In the last chapter we discussed how hard it is to believe the gospel of Jesus Christ. When you consider an eternal God, a virgin birth, or a resurrection from the dead, you are considering things that defy operational science. Science can neither confirm nor deny the supernatural (which is claimed by the Bible and particularly in respect to the gospel). Science can, however, confirm the confirmable and be a part of a solid basis for faith in the supernatural. But it cannot be an authority in itself. Therefore, those who deny Christ solely on the basis of human scientific models (secular historical science) do so on the basis of a counterfeit authority.

EXPERIENCE

Many of us can describe overwhelming experiences in our lives. For me, one of the most incredible experiences I ever had was at the birth of my first child. When Sarah was born I can remember standing with my mouth wide open just in awe and amazement at the wonder of birth. A new life, so delicate, so dependent, and so beautiful, one could just cry. I was not just amazed at my new little girl but at God's amazing brilliance as the mighty Creator of this world. The experience was joy, excitement, and wonder, and while I was looking at a little newborn baby, I felt so small. I felt insignificant in the presence of one of the marvels of my Creator.

My experience was real, and as I still look at Sarah today I am reminded of that incident often. Yet what must be understood is that my experience was based on the object or event that was in front of me. I experienced the sensation of wonder and joy because of what I witnessed. Experience is subjective (reactive to), not objective (the primary object).

People will often claim they know Christianity is real because of their experience and will claim experience as the authority. For some in the modern world of the Christian Church, experience has become the centerpiece of all faith, and whole worldwide movements have originated from it. Experiencing some major healing event, or internal emotion, or outward physical expression has been the basis on which many have tried to take the name of Christ throughout the world. This is not to say that we do not actually experience Christ in our life. Of course, for the Christian, our experience of the Holy Spirit living within us can certainly be a valid confirmation of the object of our faith. But what we must always understand is that experience is not the actual object of faith but subjective to the objective truth of God's Word.

Kel Willis, author of *The Experience Trap*, rightly says:

> A faith that is dependent and focused on spiritual experiences produces in us a constant need of something more in order to maintain the spiritual momentum of our lives. Because all experience by its very nature is transitory, an experience-centered faith results in insecurity, instability, and, frequently, disillusionment.[3]

When personal experience determines truth, many other religious groups can also claim to have "the truth." In fact, commitment to any belief system will produce an

---

3. Kel Willis, *The Experience Trap* (Australia: CGM Publishing, 1996), p. 1.

immediate sense that it is right. I recently read testimonies of Islamic women who said their faith had given them peace and contentment. Does that make Islam right? Not at all, but neither does the Christian's experience of God determine the truth of the gospel.[4]

Experience in this way is subjective to its object. Kel Willis is clearly showing here that there are experiences all over the world that are subjective to their objects of truth that contradict each other. Experience alone cannot help us to distinguish between these claimed truths.

Further in this book, we will look at how experiencing God's authority in our lives is a wonderful part of our Christian faith, but we can never claim the experience itself as the centerpiece or authority for our faith. The claim of experience, to accept or deny Christ, is to claim on the basis of a counterfeit authority.

STATE AND GOVERNMENT

Henry Morris describes *statism* as

. . . the system that regards the state as the ultimate authority and reality, so that all its youth should be educated by state-trained teachers with the primary goal of advancing the good of the state. Originating in antiquity, the statist philosophy of education was especially formalized and promoted by the Greek philosophers, notably Plato and Aristotle. In modern time, this system has been developed and followed to the extreme degree in Nazi Germany and in the various communist nations.[5]

Henry Morris was discussing statism (governmental authority) in its relationship to education and the education system. As we have seen in history, governmental authority has been vigorously

4. Ibid., p. 7.
5. Henry Morris, *Christian Education for the Real World* (Green Forest, AR: Master Books, 1977), p. 5.

abused in many nations, eliminating many freedoms. Through the years and ever since Christ, Christianity has been outlawed under the regimes of many dictators and systems (especially communist regimes and fundamentalist Muslim regimes). But for every dictator and system, the Church has survived, claiming countless martyrs along the way. For these Christians, the policies of the state were not a sufficient reason for denying the gospel of Christ.

A good read of *Foxe's Book of Martyrs* will soon give you the impression that many millions of Christians have been willing to die under oppressive regimes for the name of Christ. As an example, the book describes one of the first, Polycarp, who was a student under the Apostle John:

> After his sentence was given, the governor said to him, "Reproach Christ and I will release you." Polycarp answered, "Eighty-six years I have served Him, and He never once wronged me. How then shall I blaspheme my King who has saved me?" In the market place he was tied to the stake rather than nailed, as was the usual custom, because he assured them he would stand immovable in the flames and not fight them.[6]

In fact, history records that the flames did not burn Polycarp so he had to be speared. Polycarp's commitment to and faith in Christ was something beyond state authority.

Statism is the rule of a governing philosophy based on autonomous human reason. We have already discussed in this chapter that autonomous human reason and philosophy is at best limited and fallible. Many people have agreed with this, having been prepared to lose their lives for Christ rather than accept the state's authority. The underground church in China and Russia has grown in incredible numbers under the oppression of governments with no (or at least little) religious tolerance.

---

6. John Foxe, *The New Foxe's Book of Martyrs* (North Brunswick, NJ: Bridge-Logos Publishing, 1997), p. 16.

Throughout the history of this world it has also always been a role of government to uphold the law for that which is good (at least supposed to be). Moral law (good and evil) is unexplainable without an originator. What makes something good or bad? Who decides? If we are all here as a process of chance, why should anything be right or wrong? The fact that a government upholds moral law does not make it the originator of moral law. We need to know a base standard — the base authority.

When Jesus Himself was questioned on the basis of the authority of the state (regarding taxes) Jesus said, "Give to Caesar what is Caesar's, and to God what is God's" (Matt. 22:21; NIV). Jesus was very clearly stating that while we live within the laws of our land, there is always a higher authority. This is an authority that millions of people throughout the years have been prepared to die for rather than be forced to deny at the hands of an oppressive regime claiming counterfeit authority.

Culture / Tradition

In many parts of the world, religion is synonymous with culture. For many people living in Dublin, Ireland, to be Irish is to be Catholic. Yet for many in Northern Ireland, to be Irish is to be Protestant. For many people living in Iran, to be an Iranian is to be Islamic, and so we could continue.

Many religions have been born out of certain aspects of ancient culture. A few years ago I met a man who opened my eyes to Arabian culture and how rich it was in the arts and especially in poetry. His name is Daniel Shayesteh, and before becoming a Christian he was an Islamic fundamentalist living in Iran. In his book *The Difference Is the Son*, Daniel has this to say about some of the cultural influence in Islam:

> In pre-Islamic culture, the purpose of Arab warriors was not only to win the war, but also to gain glory for their tribe. The joy and glory of this victory led people to express the

glorification of the tribe in poems and pass from generation to generation as a mark of honor to that tribe. The poetic language was common throughout the peninsula of Arabia. . . . Mecca as the center of shrines and religious poetry played a significant role in spreading the poems through its many pilgrims to all parts of the peninsula. . . . Muhammad was a clever Arab boy, gifted in poetry.[7]

Poetic Arab culture with its rich history of warriors has had a large part to play in the origination and preservation of Islam. For Arabian people in particular, a poetic culture has given the religion of Islam a certain charm. Culture plays a huge part in the religion of Islam, and Islam itself has become a strong binding glue for many Islamic families. As more and more people make the nation of Australia their home, I see the preservation of culture all around me, and each culture has its strong characteristics. Whether it is poetry, music, food, dress, language, or customs, there is an amazing and rich diversity among the people groups of our world. It is this richness of culture bound to a religious belief that makes it so difficult to step out of, and for some who have, they have also been ostracized from their people group, and even their own families.

In this sense it is plainly visible that culture itself is not a message or teaching, but culture can certainly enrich or embrace the philosophy in which it is bound. Yet my friend Daniel has still kept his Arabian culture alive. He is a poet, he plays his Iranian stringed instrument, his wife cooks Iranian dishes, both speak in a rich and fluent language, and their hospitality (another rich aspect of Arab culture) is amazing. But now they do it all for Jesus.

For Daniel, a greater authority now shines through his cultural riches. But it is not culture or tradition in itself. That, too, would be counterfeit authority.

7. Daniel Shayesteh, *The Difference Is the Son* (Castle Hill, N.S.W.: Daniel Shayesteh, 2004), p. 37.

THERE CAN ONLY BE ONE

Whether they realize it or not, many people are taking these things that we have been talking about and using them as their authority for life. Whether it be his or her own human reason or philosophy, or someone else's, or scientific theory, or experience . . . they are all singing the same song: "I did it my way." At the end of the day, any of these positions are based on human authority. When we take these positions we are ultimately saying that we have created our own system of belief upon our own basis of authority. Counterfeit authority allows us to pick and choose whatever theory we will live by to suit our own will. Ultimately, each of the counterfeit authorities we have discussed in this chapter (and any other claims based on human authority) can be reduced to only two possibilities. Either God the Creator is the authority or it is mankind in whichever form we apply it. Everything we have discussed comes down to human authority. Can man really be the ultimate authority?

The Bible claims that there can only be one authority that is above all human authority. He is an authority that defies human reason and yet has given the very foundation of logic on the basis we are able to reason. He is an authority that in many ways defies science and yet has given us much that we can scientifically confirm, and a written history that fits with the evidence in this world. His authority is over not only our life experience but also our experience in eternity. He is the very Author of Life. The Bible also claims to be the very words of that author. If there is one claiming absolute authority over human reason, science, experience, the state, or culture and tradition, we should understand something of these claims and look into them closely. We should look closely at this authority by which we believe a gospel that is hard to believe. The claims of biblical authority matter — a great deal.

Chapter 4

Authentic: The Real Authority

The Bible claims to be an authentic and accurate message from the Creator, and it actually reads like one. The onus, therefore, is on its critics to prove otherwise.[1]
— *Brian H. Edwards*

Can man and his human reason really be the ultimate authority? Ultimately, we are all limited. None of us can claim to have unlimited power or might, knowledge or wisdom, or an eternal existence with no beginning or end. Humanity is limited in knowledge, power, and presence. Any claim of absolute authority must surely come from outside the realms of limited human capacity. When we deny Christ or His gospel on the basis of the systems we discussed in the last chapter, we do so on the basis of a limited capacity — a human capacity.

What if, however, we had an authoritative basis for our faith that was authentically authoritative? What if we could claim an authority outside the realms of time and natural law? What if we could claim an authority with unlimited capacity of presence, power, and

---

1. Brian Edwards, *Nothing but the Truth* (Darlington, UK: Evangelical Press, 2006), p. 114–115.

knowledge? If we had a claim of absolute authority in this realm, wouldn't we then be foolish to consider anything else until we had fully investigated the claims of such an authority? Wouldn't we be foolish to consider a limited human reason before we fully considered a claim of unlimited absolute authority?

The Bible claims absolute authority. It claims to be the Word of God. It claims to be without error and claims to be completely trustworthy. The Bible claims that there is no higher source of authority and that there is no higher judge. The Bible claims to be God's special revelation to mankind, the revelation and living message from our Creator. The Bible claims that the very laws that govern our world originate from God. The Bible claims that God is the final authority because He is the self-existent, eternal God who has no beginning and no end. The Bible claims that God is all-powerful, all-knowing, and ever present — unlimited, the originator, provider, and sustainer of all. Experience cannot claim this authority, neither can philosophy, government, culture, or even science. It is also irrelevant to tell God to prove it because there is no proof greater than God. We are but His creation. God has claimed authority and given us His Word that reads authoritatively. Whether we want to accept it or not, He has claimed this authority, and it is up to critics to prove otherwise. Everyone, of course, has the right to deny that the Bible is an authentic record, but we can never deny what the Bible claims to be. Bryan Edwards's book *Nothing but the Truth* is a must-read on this matter and a book I revisit regularly. He has so clearly stated, "The onus is therefore on its critics to prove otherwise."

The Bible sets itself apart from every other book and every other claim of authority. There are many books that make claims of divine inspiration, but the points that isolate the Bible from every other book are the points that make every diligent reader sit up and pay attention to its authority and the authenticity of its reading.

The Bible has been distributed more than every other book in the known world. It has been translated into more languages than every other book in the known world, and it continues to be translated at a hastening pace. It has influenced culture, arts, science, language, literature, and even music more than any other book in history. It is also a book that has been more criticized and condemned than any other in history. More people have been persecuted even unto death over this book than any other.

The Bible stands alone in having a history of writing that spans 1,600 years with contributors from different times, positions, and vocations, and with status from kings to fishermen. Even with this incredible diversity, the consistency of the message is clear and without contradiction. The Bible has a history that has been confirmed countless times through the application of observation (sciences and archaeology — see appendix). It has a distinguishable history that has a consistent logical route from origin to destination. It gives account of the real detail of history, not overlooking the more distasteful acts of humanity. It has an account of many different prophecies from many different people of many different times, all written hundreds of years before their fulfillment in Jesus Christ (see the appendix about the Dead Sea Scrolls). Archaeology is consistently making finds confirming the accuracy of the historical account of Scripture, whether it is finding a king previously unknown to the world except for one statement in the Bible or finding information about a census that confirms the same operation of census described in the Bible. Through an understanding of Scripture we can apply a logic, reason, and observation in this physical world and find that there is no match to its accuracy.

The Bible has a consistent description of the God who claims authorship. We read of the character of God in which each aspect is so overwhelmingly and consistently complemented by all other aspects of His character that it could not be initiated from human perception. Whether you are reading of God's character, or a moral issue, or teaching on love or even on the matter of salvation, there is an amazing ring of truth found within the Bible. A great way to test the authenticity of the Bible is to simply read it.

The Bible has accuracy of history, unity of message, reason of logic, a way and destination that can fill the need of every human without exception, an amazing account of prophecies that have been clearly fulfilled, consistency of description of the amazing character of God, and it has a life-changing message that rings through in the testimony of countless believers.

The Scriptures, however, are also self-authenticating, and many people do not like this consideration, but it is something that we use every day. Everyone self-authenticates when they tell us something about themselves that we don't know. Perhaps someone might tell you that they had an afternoon nap the day before. If we were not there to see it, it is up to the reputation and honesty of that person as to whether we will believe it. There is no greater reputation and honesty than what we see in the Bible and witness in God. This ultimately is God's Word, and there is no one greater than God to confirm it.

Growing up in the Ham family was an incredible experience. From an early age I can remember my father teaching me of the authority of Scripture, not from his own view, but actually showing me the verses and claims of Scripture from Scripture. Some might say that this type of "indoctrination" has not allowed me to consider any other view, but I have been able to see all of man's philosophies in the light of the only consistent and authoritative account of the history of this world there is. Yes, the truth is I am a Christian who believes the Bible as it's written (understanding the Bible as literal truth within the context and genre as it is written), and I believe steadfastly in God's authority. But I can also say that I do not do so blindly, and throughout my years now the history of the Bible has shouted God's truth to me at various times in my life. Whether it has been seeing the tragedy in this world matching the history of God's Curse on sin, or seeing the expanse of the Grand Canyon matching the history of His judgment in Genesis 6–8, or even experiencing the measure of peace and joy in my life as promised through Jesus Christ, God has continued to stamp His authority through His Word into my life.

Many people have given me reason to look further than my own upbringing in considering the biblical claims of authority. Mostly they have come to me to give me their justification for not believing in the literal six days of creation in Genesis. So often I have taken their considerations, whether they be from dating methods (such as carbon or radiometric dating), or fossil finds, or problems with genealogies. Every time I have looked seriously and closely at such considerations, I have never been able to see any fault with Scripture. In fact, I gladly accept all critics of the Bible, for they have enabled the Lord to strengthen my faith time and time again.

The Bible's claims of authority stand alone. They are made by the "I AM." He does not require anything from us to prove the credibility of His awesome authority. The very fact that we have confirmable evidence and wonderful experience is an amazing and additional blessing. It is a blessing that "tightens the hinges" or strengthens the faith of a very limited and fallible humankind.

Let's look carefully at some of the biblical claims and consider some of the impacts of these claims. As we do so, for many readers this may be the first step of tightening some of those loose hinges that we are basing our eternal beliefs on. For Blaise Pascal, thankfully, his faith was certainly based on more than the probability of his wager. Holding onto a theory such as Pascal's wager as the basis for one's faith is certainly a loose hinge, but there is a place to consider Pascal's wager. It should be considered first by acknowledging the claims of biblical authority. Under an axiom (foundational starting point) of biblical authority, Pascal's wager simply becomes a fact. God's Word claims authority. The fact is, on the basis of that claim, anyone can deny or accept God's authority. Those who reject God's authority and inevitably find themselves to be wrong have made an eternal catastrophe of their lives. The wager in itself is not the reason to become a Christian or even accept the existence of God, but certainly we should consider the authoritative claims of Scripture seriously because Scripture does indeed state eternal consequences for those who reject the saving mercy of Christ. On the basis of scriptural authority we find clearly that there are two ways to live: with God or without God. There is an eternal difference between them.

So what does Scripture itself claim in respect to authority?

THE BIBLE CLAIMS AUTHORITY ONLY FROM GOD

And so we have the prophetic word confirmed, which you do well to heed as a light that shines in a dark place, until the day dawns and the morning star rises in your hearts; knowing this first, that no prophecy of Scripture is of any private interpretation, for prophecy never came by the will of man, but holy men of God spoke as they were moved by the Holy Spirit (2 Pet. 1:19–21).

There are so many things significant about this verse. We could concentrate on the prophecy fulfilled in Christ (which we will do a little in future chapters). We could concentrate on the prophets themselves that this verse is talking about. We could look at the light of God's Word through the entire history of the world, shining through with logic and authority into the lives of countless men and women. But it would be so easy to miss the simple claim that is so deliberately resplendent in this Scripture. No prophecy (either fore-telling or forth-telling) in Scripture has come from the will of men, but from the Holy Spirit through them. The Bible clearly claims that we truly have the Word of God and not the word of men. The words of Scripture could not have been penned without the moving of the Holy Spirit in the lives of men.

If we are to truly have a revelation from the Creator of all things, surely we would expect His revelation to be trustworthy. If God's revelation is simply a creation of men, all we have is a story about God that may or may not be true. For the Bible to be a cred-ible revelation from God, it truly should be from God, and when considered that God's Word is truly God's Word, we instantly have expectation to concur with that. We would expect that God's Word is 100 percent trustworthy, 100 percent reliable, 100 per-cent credible, and 100 percent truthful. Any deviation from this is to question the trustworthiness, reliability, credibility, and truth of God's very authority.

In this Scripture we also see something happening that is in itself a proof of the work of the Holy Spirit in the life of the Apostle Peter in penning these words. Peter, you will remember, was the Apostle who was so scared of the consequences that he denied Christ three times. He also ran away and hid (with most of the other Apostles) during Jesus' crucifixion. In both of his letters we now have an undoubtedly different Peter proclaiming clearly in the introduction that he is a servant and Apostle of Jesus Christ. There is no denying that Peter is the Apostle enlightened to understand who Jesus was, but when it came to publicly proclaiming his association with Christ on the night of His arrest, Peter failed miserably. What happened to make Peter so courageous in his later ministry? We now have Peter with a new power and courage boldly proclaiming his association with Christ in his epistles. This is the very Peter whom God used to make His claim of biblical authority. Peter could not make this claim. In fact, left to his own devices, he failed miserably at claiming Christ's authority. It is God who made this claim to us previously through a person so incapable of doing so on his own. The Word of God is not from the will of men.

In his book *Why We Believe the Bible*, John MacArthur gives us some wonderful insight into how the Bible consistently and continually claims not to be from the will of men but from the origination of God. He states:

> If the Bible is infallible and inerrant, it must be our final word — our highest stand of authority. The writers of the Old Testament make more than 2,000 direct claims to be speaking the very words of God. Again and again they wrote such phrases as "the Spirit of the Lord has spoken to me" or "the Word of God came unto me." For example, Isaiah opens his prophecy by saying, "Hear, O heavens! Listen, O earth! For the Lord has spoken" (Isa. 1:2). When

God speaks, everybody is to listen because He is the final authority.[2]

THE BIBLE CLAIMS THAT ALL SCRIPTURE IS FROM GOD

And that from childhood you have known the Holy Scriptures, which are able to make you wise for salvation through faith which is in Christ Jesus. All Scripture is given by inspiration of God, and is profitable for doctrine, for reproof, for correction, for instruction in righteousness, that the man of God may be complete, thoroughly equipped for every good work (2 Tim. 3:15–17).

In direct correlation with our point above, we again have a statement from the Apostle Paul in this verse telling us that Scripture is given by the inspiration of God. Actually, the Apostle Paul has made it very clear in this statement. The Greek word used for "inspiration" in this verse is *theopneustos*, which is made up of two Greek words: *theos* (God) and *pneuma* (spirit, breath, or wind). So in this passage, this inspiration of God means that He breathed out His Word through men. In their writings we see evidence of their human personalities and even historical research that they did (e.g., Luke 1:1–3). But God so worked through Peter and Paul that what they wrote is exactly what He wanted, and it was without error.

Even more than this, in the above verse from Timothy, Paul is telling us that God's Word is not confined to some parts of the Bible, but the whole of the Scriptures is God's Word. *ALL Scripture is God-breathed.* Yet some are not willing to accept this, claiming that the Bible merely *contains* God's Word.

In his work *The Voice of Authority*, George W. Marston comments on the folly of such a consideration:

Among those who reject the Bible as the Word of God are some who recognize that the Bible contains the Word of God. At first glance these men might seem to have a

2. John MacArthur, *Why Believe the Bible?* 2nd edition (Ventura, CA: Regal Books, 2007), p. 16.

God-given standard in matters of faith and practice but what do they mean by this statement? Simply this, that while some of the Bible is the Word of God, much of it is not. Certain truths are to be found in the Scriptures, truths that God has revealed in nature, truths which for the most part are to be found in other religions. These truths and perhaps others have been discovered by the writers of the Bible. Such truths must, however, be winnowed from the chaff of fiction, fable, legend, symbolism and history in which they were embedded and preserved by these writers of the past.

If the Bible only contains the Word of God, how can we be certain as to what is the Word of God and what is not? The identity of the word, the acceptance or rejection of certain statements as the word of God becomes a matter of opinion. Therefore the Bible cannot be regarded as an authoritative standard. It is man who determines what is the Word of God. It is man who determines what is his final authority in matters of truth and conduct. In reality, man is his own authority.[3]

Apart from accepting the entire canon of Scripture as God's Word, there is no other possible claim of authority in this world that can credibly claim authenticity. It can come from no human philosophy, government, institution, or establishment. Not even the Church can claim an authority outside Scripture, for the Church is made of fallible humans. Martin Luther was one who recognized this, much to the disgust and opposition of the established Church at the time. When asked where religious authority lies, Luther replied, "Not in the visible institution called the Roman church but in the Word of God found in the Bible."[4] It was this return to the Word of God as the complete and sole authority that has brought millions of lost people to salvation.

---

3. George Marston, *The Voice of Authority* (Phillipsburg, NJ: Presbyterian and Reformed Publ. Co., 1960), p. 32.
4. Bruce L. Shelly, *Church History in Plain English* (Dallas, TX: Word Publishing, 1995), p. 246.

As you read through both the Old and New Testaments, you will see claims of God's authority and inspiration consistently throughout His Word. It is undeniably visible and deliberate. It is not up to man to decide how we are going to determine if the Bible is wholly the Word of God or only *contains* the Word of God. The Bible systematically and consistently claims to be the Word of God. We read contributions from prophets, priests, kings, apostles, and those closely associated, all understating their own importance and attributing the message to that of God and Christ. If there are people claiming that the Bible is partly God's Word or may contain God's Word, they make a claim opposing the claims that the Bible makes about itself.

Dr. Martin Lloyd-Jones made this clear, as he has asked us to consider our fallible view of Scripture compared to Scripture's view of itself:

> Who decides what is true? Who decides what is of value? How can you discriminate and differentiate between the great facts that are true and those that are false? How can you differentiate and separate facts from teaching? How can you separate this essential message of the Bible from the background in which it is presented? . . . The whole Bible comes to us and offers itself to us in exactly the same way. There is no hint, no suspicion of a suggestion that parts of it are important and parts are not. They all come to us in the same form.[5]

THE RELIABILITY OF SCRIPTURAL AUTHORITY

There are many reasons we can assert that the Bible is the credible source of authority for the world today. It is not just on the basis that physical evidence matches the historical record of Scripture. It's also not simply on the basis that experience shows a testimonial evidence of a Christ-changed life. Although these are helpful tools providing some basis for faith, real reliability in authority is self-testifying (as per the claims above) and logically so. We have clearly

---

5. MacArthur, *Why Believe the Bible?* p. 18, quote from Dr. D.M. Lloyd-Jones, "The Authority of Scripture," *Eternity*, 1957.

seen that only God can be a fit witness of Himself and therefore the claims of Scripture come as a foundational base for truth and the onus is on the critic to prove otherwise. Even in saying so, we must consider authority from the very source of the claim. The source claimed is God.

This is what the Westminster Confession of Faith has to say about the source of authority: "The authority of the Holy Scripture, for which it ought to be believed and obeyed, dependeth not upon the testimony of any man or church, but wholly upon God (who is truth itself), the author thereof; and therefore it is to be believed, because it is the word of God" (WCF,1/iv).

Author and biblical scholar Robert Reymond has described it this way:

> This article, explaining the ground of the Bible's author-ity, first states the ground where in the Bible's authority does not reside in the testimony of any person or church respect-ing the Bible. For any person or church to insist that people should believe and obey the Bible because of their testi-mony is to ground its authority in the opinion of fallible men. Then the article states the sole reason why the Bible ought to be believed and obeyed: because God, who is truth itself, is in a unique sense its author and therefore because it is the very Word of the one living and true God.[6]

The Bible starts with God. It self-testifies this and tells us about the One who makes this testimony. The Bible testifies that God is far beyond human capability. All through Scripture we read that God is infinite, all-powerful, all-knowing, and ever-present. He is pure, holy, righteous, and perfect, without blemish. God cannot sin. The logical expectation is that such a God is also perfectly reli-able, credible, and truthful. One only has to read the Ten Com-mandments to see this nature of God revealed in His behavioral

---

6. Dr. Robert Reymond, *The New Systematic Theology for the Christian Church* (Nashville, TN: Thomas Nelson, 1998), p. 73.

expectation of mankind. It is simply not logical to think that when a perfect, holy God commands mankind not to lie (and other moral dictates) that He would be issuing such commands from an inconsistent position, when the Bible consistently points to His righteous and holy character. When we match what the Bible says about God's character and its self-authenticating claims of authenticity, we have a basis of authority that comes from the highest possible source, with the highest possible credibility. This is why the onus is on the critic to prove otherwise. It is illogical for creatures to expect the creator to prove Himself. He has no need to bow to our demands of proof when doing so would diminish the credibility of His total and undisputed authority.

The claims of Scripture, both about God's character and Scripture itself, allow us to make two rational conclusions. The Bible must be inerrant and infallible. These two words are very important words when it comes to biblical authority. In 1978, 200 evangelical church leaders concerned about the Church's commitment to biblical authority came together to define these words and how they apply to biblical authority. This resulted in the Chicago Statement on Biblical Inerrancy and defined infallibility and inerrancy as follows:

> "Infallible" signifies the quality of neither misleading nor being misled and so safeguards in categorical terms the truth that Holy Scripture is a sure, safe, and reliable rule and guide in all matters. Similarly, "inerrant" signifies the quality of being free from all falsehood or mistake and so safeguards the truth that Holy Scripture is entirely true and trustworthy in all its assertions.[7]

On the basis of Scripture we can certainly assert that a God of perfect character breathed out His Word in inspiration (*theopneustos*) to reveal Himself through the special revelation of the Bible that we can therefore determine as being infallible and inerrant (reliable and without error) to the degree that it is our absolute, sole, and sufficient

---

7. www.en.wikisource.org/wiki/Chicago_Statement_on_Biblical_Inerrancy.

authority. This has been helpfully depicted in the following diagram drawn by Roger Patterson from Answers in Genesis.

God's
Character

▼

Inspiration:
Theopneustos

▼

Inerrancy

Infallibility

▼

Authority of Scripture:
Sole and Sufficient

There are many evangelical leaders and scholars who would strongly advocate for the infallibility and inerrancy of Scripture. Yet there is also a problem. Many of these leaders (including some who have signed the Chicago Statement on Inerrancy) have, in practice, compromised the inerrancy of Scripture by giving human philosophical positions equal standing in the assessment of God's work. This has been particularly prominent in long-age positions taken in Genesis 1 and 2. Because most secular scientists assess all historical positions on the basis of a long age agenda and the presupposition that the present dictates the past, many theologians (even good theologians) have been persuaded (or academically pressured) to include these positions in their interpretation of the biblical creation account.

Rather than commencing with the consideration of God's character, we see that physical evidence has taken the first position of assessment. This is called evidentialism, and from this the application of secular science philosophy has been input into the interpretation of Scripture. While many of these leaders and scholars would still accept the truth of God's character and the concepts of infallibility and inerrancy, they have not understood how the evidentialist approach has compromised the authority of God's Word. In this way, they have changed the previous diagram as follows.

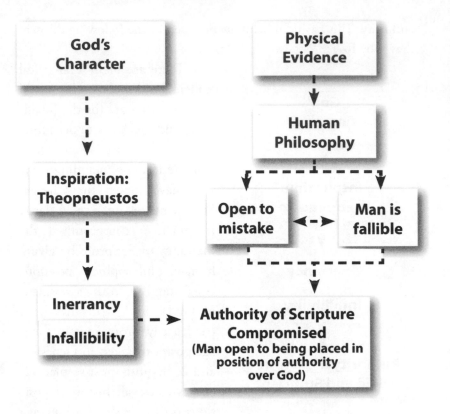

Sometimes it is at this point where I may be accused of rejecting science altogether, and neither is this a position that any Christian should take. This is especially true considering that the laws that govern scientific observation have their origin in God. There definitely should be a consideration of evidence. The final flow chart on the following page gives us the correct position for evidence in the acceptance of true biblical authority.

We have really only dealt with two amazing claims of Scripture, and while we are limited to that in this chapter, they give us the epitome of scriptural claim. Not only that, but from these claims we come to logical conclusions about the reliability of Scripture — that we have an inerrant and infallible Bible that truly is our sole and sufficient authority.

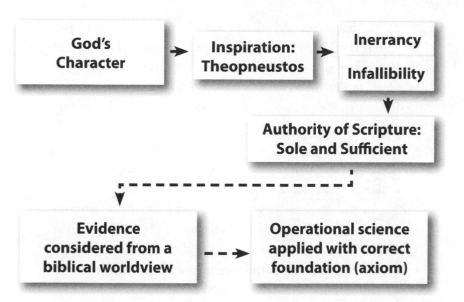

We have God's Word, not in part but as a whole. Everything God has desired to reveal to us in written word is in the Bible. He has given us His book and blessed us through conserving His Word from the start to the finish. He has given us this revelation so that we might know Him and the power of His Word for salvation in Jesus Christ. We may want to add or take from Scripture to give us more acceptance of His Word, but we would be doing so at our own peril. We cannot make fallible what is already the infallible. We would be reducing the trustworthiness of what is already the inerrant.

The first step of tightening the hinges of your faith must therefore be an acceptance of the authority of Scripture. We can rely on the total message within because of whom it is from. It is from the almighty, unlimited God, the "I AM."

Given his outstanding work in relation to the authority and inspiration of Scripture, I am going to let Brian Edwards have the last say in this chapter:

> In 1632 the Italian scientist Galileo published a book in which he supported the view of Copernicus a century

earlier that the earth is round and that the sun is the center of our solar system. The church authorities disagreed and his book was banned. Galileo was forced to renounce his views under threat of death by the infamous Inquisition. In fact, Galileo was right and he knew he was right; merely declaring him to be in error and forcing him to change his views altered nothing of the truth. Today any school children who learn about Galileo know what the great mathematician and astronomer really believed.

In the same way, we cannot read the Bible without coming to the conclusion that what it claims for itself is an authority that allows nothing higher. No other writings, no other documents, and the views of no other teachers or philosophers are ever referred to in the Bible as carrying the same authority. Some of our great philosophers and religious leaders were alive in Bible times, including Plato, who was born 400 years before Christ, and Gautama the founder of Buddhism, who was born a century before Plato, but they are never mentioned and certainly never quoted in Scripture. To the human writers of the Bible, both in the Old and New Testaments, there is only one authoritative Scripture.

Like the authorities in Italy who punished Galileo for telling the truth, critics may not like what the Bible says about itself. They may even consider it to be wrong. But what they must never do is to pretend that it does not claim such a clear authority for itself. We may twist its words and change its meaning, but like the views of Galileo, the whole world will know what the Bible really teaches about itself. Willful unbelief, ignorance, or fear of accepting the claims of the Bible can never change the truth of them.[8]

God's authority matters, and it matters a great deal.

---

8. Edwards, *Nothing but the Truth*, p. 114–115.

Chapter 5

Axiom: A Basis of Authority

When the plain sense of Scripture makes common sense, seek no other sense; therefore take every word at its primary, ordinary, usual, literal meaning unless the facts of the immediate text, studied in the light of related passages and axiomatic and fundamental truths, clearly indicate otherwise.[1] — *Dr. David L. Cooper*

ax·i·om

1. a self-evident truth that requires no proof
2. a universally accepted principle or rule
3. logic, mathematics; a proposition that is assumed without proof for the sake of studying the consequences that follow from it[2]

A xiom is a word used only in unique circumstances. It is an axiomatic principle that it is impossible for something to both exist and not exist at the same time. It is a principle that requires no proof. For the purpose of this chapter, we will define the word *axiom* as a self-evident truth that requires no proof. It is important to consider the

---

1. www.biblicalresearch.info/page7.html, "Rules of Interpretation."
2. www.dictionary.com.

difference between requiring no proof and an inability to be proven. As we look at evidence through the eyes of Scripture we can make complete and confirming sense of the evidence in this world, and so Scripture does not require blind faith. It is vital to understand that Scripture is our starting foundation in all matters and the very center of our thinking with great confirmability. It is only in this manner that I use the words *axiom* and *presupposition* interchangeably. As we discovered in the last chapter, the Bible makes very clear statements about itself. The Bible is from God, not man, and all of it is from God. The Bible makes this statement and requires no proof. God is God and whether we want to attempt to prove it or not does not discount the fact that He is. His word is the authority, and whether or not we want to prove or disprove it, it is. It is an added blessing that we are even able to confirm it, and as we look at this world through the eyes of Scripture, it really does make perfect sense.

Anyone reading the Bible or taking it even half seriously would have to come across the claims of scriptural authority, and when we do it puts us in a unique situation. To look at the world we can only consider Scripture with integrity when we apply its own principles. As God's Word, Scripture claims to be the first and final authority. Our axiom must then be that God's authoritative Word must be both the first and final source of truth. We might not like that (and most don't), but it does not change the fact that it is. When we look, therefore, at the things in this world, we must consider the most logical starting point. It must be and can only be God's Word. It is from this point that we see and assess the world we live in through biblical vision.

Maybe you are now starting to have some concern with what I am saying. You are recognizing a bias and this is starting to concern you. We should therefore ask a question: is it possible to consider anything without bias? My answer is no. We either look at this world with a bias of biblical authority or we look at this world with a bias of man's authority. At the end of the day, it depends on which bias is the best bias to be biased by. Particularly when considering the area of origins (historical science), neutrality is a false claim. You either accept that God was there and assess the evidence according to His written history or you base your assessment on man's philosophical assumptions (millions of years of evolution).

One of the first things you will learn when you study biblical theology is the concept of general and *special* revelation. God has revealed Himself in general ways through the creation around us, through our moral and religious sense, through the constant natural laws that give us logic, mathematics, physics, etc. These are the things that as human beings we see and wonder how they can be. Where does natural law have its origin, or where did the very world and universe we live in come from? Where does a sense of good and evil come from and how come the whole world through religion is looking for God and meaning to life? General revelation really does lead us to questions, but those questions without a specific foundation of interpretation are truly unanswerable.

We have, however, obtained God's special revelation in two major ways. He has revealed Himself through His Word and He has revealed Himself through the Incarnation. Giving consideration to Jesus and the Bible is the best way of interpreting the world and life in which we live. The most important issue to understand about general and special revelation is that it is impossible to understand general revelation without the interpretation of special revelation. From the beginning of history, mankind has required special revelation to interpret general revelation. Cornelius Van Til was one of the greatest scholars in the field of apologetics and the understanding of the evidence in general revelation. He refers to the very beginning of humanity in this way: "God's revelation in nature was from the outset of history meant to be taken conjointly with God's supernatural Communications."[3] Van Til was referring to Genesis 2 and the explicit account of the sixth day of creation. In the Garden of Eden, Adam was given explicitly communicated instructions from God in relation to understanding the environment around him. In

---

3. Tom Notaro, *Van Til and the Use of Evidence* (Phillipsburg, NJ: Presbyterian and Reformed Publishing Company, 1980), p. 49.

the midst of the beautiful garden surrounding him, God supernaturally instructed Adam to work it and keep it, to eat of any of the trees except the tree of the knowledge of good and evil.

God's special revelation allowed Adam to make sense of the environment around him, otherwise he had no way on his own but to imagine and guess. When we choose to reject God's special revelation for understanding the world around us and the life we live, we also simply imagine and guess, much like one of Adam's most famous descendents — Charles Darwin. The fact that Charles Darwin had rejected the idea that he was a descendent of the literal Adam doesn't alter the fact that he was. When Charles Darwin viewed the general revelation of creation by looking at natural selection and speciation, he chose to ignore God's special revelation in Genesis that gives us the boundary for change being within each kind. Charles Darwin had a starting point of naturalism (nature is all there is) rather than special creation (nature is subservient to God).

One of the greatest errors in the world of theology is the idea of some that the authority of God's Word only encompasses the realms of morality, religious understanding, and issues regarding our relationship with God. We find people making wonderful statements about the authority of the Bible, but the definition of authority is confined to matters of faith and conduct. This is not only a limitation of the Bible's authority, but it is also a rejection of the unlimited authority of God. These authoritative rejection statements can come in many different forms. They can sometimes sound something like this: "The Bible is not a scientific textbook." We may all accept that the Bible claims to be the God-breathed, special revelation to man. We also agree in general that there is some truth in the fact that the Bible is not simply a scientific textbook. Statements like these, however, are sometimes made to imply that the Bible has no authority at all in the realms of science, archaeology, psychology, philosophy, etc. If God is the author and God is unlimited, then the accurate description of the Bible is as follows. The Bible is the final authority in every single matter in which it deals, for it is the Word of God. If

the Bible contradicts man's opinion in biology, anthropology, astronomy, archaeology, geology, psychology, or philosophy, then we must
immediately assume that mankind's idea is incorrect in the light of
the unlimited, eternal, omniscient God.

The point to be made in all of this discussion is that an acceptance of God and the claims of His Word means that it is illogical to commence any research on any matter until you first accept
God as the first and final authority in relation to it. We therefore
must start with Scripture and see all there is to see through the great
viewing glass that is God's Word. This should be every Christian's
great presupposition. Our axiomatic basis is that God's Word is our
authoritative starting point for all matters. Too many of our brothers and sisters in Christ have started with what they call a neutral
position and placed man as the authority and then attempted to fit
man's authority into the Bible. Every human being, at some stage,
is somewhat guilty of idolatry, and this is another form. That mankind's "neutral" interpretation of evidence can be the starting point
prior to God's Word can only be described as a form of idolatry.
There is no such thing as neutrality. There is only the worshiping
of ourselves over our Creator and putting our authority above His.
This is why my father placed the quote from Dr. David L. Cooper
(at the heading of this chapter) in the first page of his Bible.

Christians also specifically believe strongly in the Lordship of
Jesus Christ. We love to call Him Lord, to teach that He is Lord,
to sing of His lordship, to proclaim and rely on His victory over
death and sin. We proclaim Him as the center of our lives and the
very meaning of our existence. We believe John 1 where we are told
that Jesus is the Word, that He was with God, and that He is God.
The Word is the light, the life, the Creator, and the incarnate God
who lived among us and made atonement for our sin. It is Jesus,
the Son, who has amazing authority. The Apostle Paul tells us in
Colossians 2:3 that it is in the Father and in Christ "in whom are
hidden all the treasures of wisdom and knowledge." Jesus our Lord
and Savior is not limited to matters of faith and conduct, but to

all-encompassing matters of wisdom and knowledge. He is omniscient. Paul then goes on to discuss what it means to be walking with Christ and to be rooted and built up in Him and to be established in the faith. In the middle of this discussion Paul gives us a clear warning in verse 8: "Beware lest anyone cheat you through philosophy and empty deceit, according to the tradition of men, according to the basic principles of the world, and not according to Christ" (Col. 2:8).

Greg Bahnsen, in his book *Always Ready*, puts the case of neutrality (in respect to Christ's authority) this way in reference to Colossians 2:8:

> By attempting to be neutral in your thought you are a prime target for being robbed — robbed by "vain philosophy" of all the treasures of "wisdom and knowledge" which are deposited in Christ alone. Paul explains that vain philosophy is that which follows the world and not Christ; it is this thinking that submits to the world's demand for neutrality rather than being presuppositionally committed to Christ in all of our thinking.
>
> Are you rich in knowledge because of your commitment to Christ in scholarship, apologetics, and schooling, or have you been robbed by the demands of neutrality?[4]

Bahnsen further states, "Consequently, when the Christian approaches scholarship, apologetics, or schooling he must staunchly refuse to acquiesce to the mistaken demands of neutrality in his life; he must never consent to surrender his distinctive religious beliefs 'for the time being' as though one might thereby arrive at genuine knowledge 'impartially.' The beginning of Knowledge is the fear of the Lord (Prov. 1:7)."[5]

The point is simple, and yet many still do not fully grasp the ramifications of this point. We can only serve one master at a time

4. Greg Bahnsen, *Always Ready*, 8th printing (Texarkana, AR: Covenant Media Press, 2007), p. 5.
5. Ibid., p. 6.

— either God or man. It is not consistent with Christ's lordship to suggest that in one matter we place His authority aside for our own.

The axiomatic approach stands on the claims of Scripture first, with the foundation that God's Word is already the full, sole, and final authority. The evidentialist position, while often in agreement with the principle that God's Word is the authority, is also an attempt to interpret Scripture on the basis of how a supposed neutral assessment of the evidence determines the meaning of the passage being read. The problem is that a "neutral" assessment is never really neutral. At some stage, autonomous human reasoning is adapted as part of the interpretative method, rather than Scripture being the foundation for the interpretation of evidence.

As an example, some from an evidentialist approach have come to the conclusion that human death, as a consequence for sin, can only be a spiritual rather than a physical death. This position has been adopted by and large to account for the popular belief that death has been in existence before man, as illustrated by a fossil record that supposedly precedes man by millions of years.

The scope and definition of "death" as a consequence of sin is determined by the reader's approach being "axiomatic" or "evidential." It is an important issue because the Bible tells us that "the wages of sin is death" (Rom. 6:23). The Bible also tells us in Romans 5:12 and 17 that we have salvation through one Man's death (Jesus) and that this has saved us from the death consequence of one man's sin (Adam).

The difference between an axiomatic position and an evidentialist one in relation to the subject of "death" as a consequence of sin is real and has real ramifications in the way we assess both our need for Christ and the impact of His death on the Cross. Ultimately, it is an issue relating to the authority of Scripture itself.

The only consistent understanding of the gospel comes from an axiomatic approach. This approach allows the reader to know that physical (and spiritual) death is only normal because we live in a sin-cursed world. Death is our enemy: "The last enemy that will be destroyed is death" (1 Cor. 15:26). It is a consequence of sin that has separated us from God and His designed purpose for our lives to glorify Him. We then find perfect consistency in Jesus as the sinless sacrifice, dying and then rising to conquer death — so that in Him we can have life. We can have confidence knowing that Christ will one day restore all things back to the perfection of His original creation where there will again be no death nor suffering and perfect union with our Creator: "And God will wipe away every tear from their eyes; there shall be no more death, nor sorrow, nor crying. There shall be no more pain, for the former things have passed away" (Rev. 21:4).

Even so, there are still many from the evidentialist camp who have recognized that human death prior to sin is a direct contradiction with Romans 5 (and other similar Scriptures). As a result, these people, still maintaining an evidentialist approach, have asserted that the death consequence in Genesis 3 must be of a physical nature but restricted to humanity — not animals. One of the main reasons for this is that the fossil record contains billions of animal fossils, supposedly (as the secularists claim) laid down millions of years before humans came into existence. From the evidentialists' perspective, they then assert that when the Bible talks of death as a result of sin, it is only talking of human death. In this way, the evidentialist approach has already placed a human belief system as the authority in interpreting Scripture rather than allowing Scripture to give us the framework of assessing the fossil record evidence. To support their philosophical input into the text of Genesis, many further assert that the beginning chapters of Genesis are poetic (or mythological) rather than literal history.

In an attempt to be neutral, the evidentialist has assessed the evidence with a presupposition of "millions of years," which then becomes the basis of assessment before even considering that Scripture itself may have a perfectly logical and historical explanation for the evidence of the fossil record. In other words, man's wisdom is placed above God's.

Those with an axiomatic approach respect scriptural authority for the answers to these evidentialist conclusions. For instance, consider the following passages that together enable a truly biblical (axiomatic) approach to this subject:

> Then God saw everything that He had made, and indeed it was very good. So the evening and the morning were the sixth day (Gen. 1:31).

God created a world without disorder. The infinite, perfect God looked at His creation at the end of the sixth day and described it as very good. It is a totally incorrect notion to consider a creation built upon layers of death and suffering over millions of years as very good in the eyes of a pure and holy God.

> And God said, "See, I have given you every herb that yields seed which is on the face of all the earth, and every tree whose fruit yields seed; to you it shall be for food. Also, to every beast of the earth, to every bird of the air, and to everything that creeps on the earth, in which there is life, I have given every green herb for food"; and it was so (Gen. 1:29–30).

Prior to the Fall (when mankind rejected God's rule for our own kingship), all living creatures and mankind were vegetarian. As there is evidence of carnivorous activity preserved in the fossil record, the fossil record must be post-Fall. Therefore, the evidence of all associated animal death in that same fossil record logically must be post-sin.

> In the sweat of your face you shall eat bread till you return to the ground, for out of it you were taken; for dust you are, and to dust you shall return (Gen. 3:19).

> Therefore, just as through one man sin entered the world, and death through sin, and thus death spread to all men, because all sinned (Rom. 5:12).

Only after the Fall, as a consequence of sin, does God say to man that he will go back to dust (physical death). This is again emphasized in Romans 5 where we all suffer death through one man, and through one man's sinless death on a Cross we all have access to eternal life.

> Both thorns and thistles it shall bring forth for you, and you shall eat the herb of the field (Gen. 3:18).

The fossil record has many examples of fossil thorns supposedly millions of years old (millions of years before man), yet the Bible tells us that thorns are only as a result of sin. Therefore, the fossil record must be post-sin and the evidence of animal death in that same fossil record must be post-sin.

> For the creation was subjected to futility, not willingly, but because of Him who subjected it in hope; because the creation itself also will be delivered from the bondage of corruption into the glorious liberty of the children of God. For we know that the whole creation groans and labors with birth pangs together until now (Rom. 8:20–22).

Sin corrupted the entire creation of God. Therefore it is only consistent to consider that all living things are also subject to death and suffering caused by our sin. To suggest that the consequence of sin has only affected humanity is to reject that the Bible teaches that everything has been sin-cursed. We live in a sin-cursed world, not just a sin-cursed humanity.

> The waters prevailed fifteen cubits upward, and the mountains were covered. And all flesh died that moved on the earth (Gen. 7:20–21).

The most appropriate explanation for most of the fossil record comes from understanding that the entire world was once destroyed by water. The fossil record is global and the fact that the waters covered every mountaintop is consistent with a global fossil record.

> So He destroyed all living things which were on the face of the ground: both man and cattle, creeping thing and bird of the air. They were destroyed from the earth. Only Noah and those who were with him in the ark remained alive (Gen. 7:23).

Again, every living thing on the planet was destroyed (apart from the inhabitants of the ark). Further reading on the fossil record is recommended and well explained in *The New Answers Book 2* from Master Books.

> Let them praise the name of the LORD, for He commanded and they were created (Ps. 148:5).

The Bible explains how God created, not the fossil record. God created miraculously by His command. He is truly God. There is no sufficient natural explanation for the power of God. And God said . . . and it was good.

> And He answered and said to them, "Have you not read that He who made them at the beginning 'made them male and female,' and said, 'For this reason a man shall leave his father and mother and be joined to his wife, and the two shall become one flesh'?" (Matt. 19:4–5).

> For in six days the LORD made the heavens and the earth, the sea, and all that is in them, and rested the seventh day. Therefore the LORD blessed the Sabbath day and hallowed it (Exod. 20:11).

In Exodus, God refers to His creative work of Genesis 1 when giving the command for the Sabbath day law. In Matthew 19, Jesus refers directly to the words of Genesis 1 and 2 in relation to marriage. These references refer to a literal historic event, and Jesus specifically refers to Genesis, quoting it in a historical context. The biblical reference to Genesis is of an historical nature. Scripture itself accepts and refers to Genesis as an authentic historical genre.

The following diagrams give an overview of the difference in the evidentialist approach compared to the axiomatic approach in relation to the issue of death as a consequence of sin.

The final genuine question therefore to ask is, "Does evidence have a place?" Indeed yes. The use of evidence is one of the greatest blessings that God has given us. He has graciously given us an

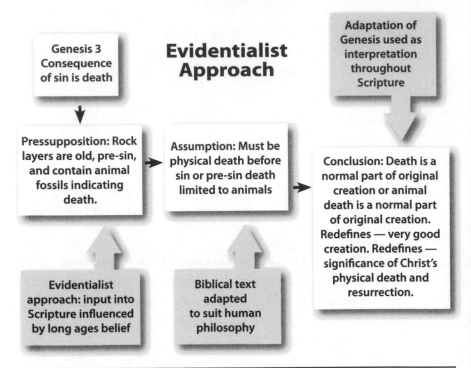

Evidentialist Approach

Genesis 3 Consequence of sin is death

Adaptation of Genesis used as interpretation throughout Scripture

Pressupposition: Rock layers are old, pre-sin, and contain animal fossils indicating death.

Assumption: Must be physical death before sin or pre-sin death limited to animals

Conclusion: Death is a normal part of original creation or animal death is a normal part of original creation. Redefines — very good creation. Redefines — significance of Christ's physical death and resurrection.

Evidentialist approach: input into Scripture influenced by long ages belief

Biblical text adapted to suit human philosophy

historical account in His Word that can be confirmed by proper interpretation of the evidence of this world. The point we all need to keep in mind, however, is that regardless of the evidence, it does not change the fact that God is the authority. But the truth is that the evidence does indeed confirm the historical accuracy of Scripture. There is a place for evidence, but evidence itself is not the authority, and based on this understanding there is no place for neutrality. We must be very careful about evidence, because many people have made evidence their starting point instead of the Bible. (Refer to diagrams in chapter 4.)

Ken Ham has stated this well in an Answers in Genesis article:

> Some who superficially read the Bible claim that Proverbs 26:4–5 makes contradictory statements: "Do not answer a fool according to his folly, lest you also be like him. Answer a fool according to his folly, lest he be wise in his own eyes."

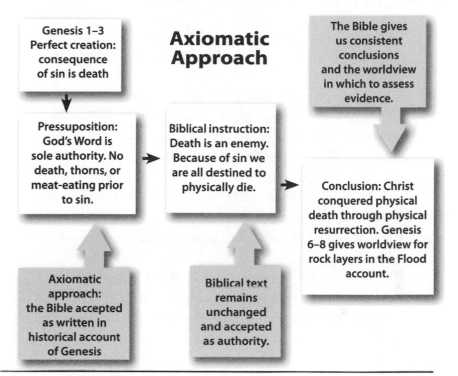

However, there are wise principles in these verses, lessons which would help Christians to be much more effective in countering false arguments and in witnessing.

Let's look at verse 4: "Do not answer a fool according to his folly, lest you also be like him."

As we have often said, one must understand that all evidence is interpreted on the basis of "presupposition." As Christians, all of our thinking — in every area — should be built upon the history revealed in God's Word. Doing this, you have the correct "big picture" way of understanding the universe so that the evidence of the present can be interpreted correctly.

Sadly, many Christians often succumb to the non-Christian's challenge to provide evidence for the existence of God, creation, the Christian faith, etc., without using the Bible.

When you agree to these terms of the debate, however, you are answering a person "according to [i.e., within the terms of] his folly."

By accepting the non-Christian's presuppositions (that thinking is not to be built on the Bible), one only has, by default, the non-Christian's way of thinking to interpret the evidence. With no true foundation (God's Word) on which to correctly (and differently) interpret the evidence, one cannot "win" the argument. Understanding the presuppositional nature of the argument, one will not answer someone "according to their folly" (i.e., based on secular presuppositions about life).

Now verse 5: "Answer a fool according to his folly, lest he be wise in his own eyes." As mentioned, on the surface, this seems to contradict verse 4. But when you think about it, there is infinite wisdom behind it.

As said, first you show the non-Christian that you will not argue according to someone else's presuppositions. Rather, you use the biblical foundation of history to interpret evidence, confirming this with real science.[6]

Ken is saying clearly that we cannot use evidence to help us interpret history, as this is the wrong way around (folly). We must use the authoritative historical foundation of Scripture to enable us to interpret evidence (and answer from the Bible in reference to the folly).

Unfortunately, there are many fine Christians who start with the evidence to consider the accuracy of Scripture. This is a denial of the authority of God as it applies to all knowledge. As we have previously considered from Proverbs 1:7 (and also in Colossians 2:2–3), "The fear of the Lord is the beginning of knowledge." We must continually remind ourselves that the only reliable God-honoring position of worshiping His lordship comes from a presuppositional stance that biblical authority is our axiom and therefore starting

---

6. www.answersingenesis.org/creation/v26/i4/answer.asp Article Ken Ham. Don't answer, Do Answer.

point for all matters of wisdom and knowledge. In this way we can truly understand with a more full and complete view what Paul wrote to Timothy when he stated that the Scriptures are to make us wise for salvation. The consistency of God's authority in Scripture from Genesis 1 to Revelation 22 helps us to more fully and consistently comprehend the lordship of Christ and wonder of the Cross.

A few years ago I was at a conference where people were asking questions of the speakers about why the Church has become so out of touch with the average Australian citizen. Sitting next to me, my brother David asked the speakers if they thought the lack of engagement of the Church with the general population was because the Church had lost its way in being able to answer Australians' questions in relation to origins and the Bible, science and the Bible, death and suffering, etc. I forget exactly how David asked the question, but I remember exactly the words used by the speakers to answer it. It was a classic answer that we Aussies would term as "letting it go through to the keeper." A wicket *keeper* in the sport of cricket is like a catcher in baseball. It is saying that the batsman let the ball go through to the keeper. I could see that they didn't want to truly answer the question because it was a too-hard basket issue for them. But when they did eventually answer, it was memorable. "We are to take Genesis seriously, but not literally." In other words, there are other issues such as evolution, long ages, and human philosophy that we cannot reconcile with the Bible, so we choose to let the world have its own authority on those issues and just preach Christ.

There is the great problem with a denial of authority. It creates a disengaged world because the Church has no answers; a world that is actually not ready to hear the message of Christ because of the inconsistency of Christians. And let us never forget that the true message of the gospel of Christ is actually a message that is hard to believe. An acceptance of God's authority in these issues, however, provides wonderful answers to a world lost in the illusion of evolutionary thinking. We have answers for fossils, dinosaurs, rock layers, dating methods, races, and why there is death and suffering in the world.

God in His great authority and omniscience has given us the ability to confirm much of the confirmable that is in His Word. We don't need to lose any scientific credibility in a literal reading of biblical history starting with the first 11 chapters of Genesis because we can use the same operational science in the confirmation of the Bible's historical accuracy. We also need not fear losing any theological academic credibility for accepting a straightforward reading of Genesis chapters 1–11 as literal history because we understand from Colossians that God does not want us to be robbed by anti-God human philosophy. And while we can actually help people see the wonder of biblical authority and the credibility of the gospel through confirming evidence, none of this confirmation even slightly changes the fact that He is indeed the first and final authority in all matters anyway.

In the appendix there is a brief overview of some of the wonderful confirmations of biblical history. Each of the areas looked at could be an entire book in itself, and you will find, in fact, that they are. So there are also some recommendations of various books you can obtain to read further in relation to confirming the confirmable.

In reference to the non-confirmable, Deuteronomy 29:29 states: "The secret things belong to the LORD our God, but those things which are revealed belong to us and to our children forever, that we may do all the words of this law."

My axiomatic principle at work finds that God tells us we won't be able to confirm everything in this world, as some things are for the moment His secret. But He also tells us He has given us more than enough to show us the aspects of His revelation that are confirmable in this world. We are not to keep these to ourselves but use them to train our children.

Is your axiom one of true presuppositional biblical authority? Do you need to repent from being an evidentialist? On behalf of a world disengaged from the gospel of Christ, I ask you to consider it. Authority matters, and it matters a great deal.

Section Two

The Authority of God

Chapter 6

Authority and God the Father

I AM WHO I AM.
— God (Exod. 3:14)

H ave you ever had anyone say to you that they have trouble believing in God because they cannot understand the Trinity? I have. How do you answer a question like that? Because, I don't understand it either. Sure, I accept and believe all that the Bible says about God, including that He is one God and that the Father is God, the Son is God, and the Holy Spirit is God, but there is only one God. In fact, God made that very clear to the Israelites in the first four of the Ten Commandments. In Exodus 20, He reminds us through the Law that He is God and that we are not to have any other gods. We are not to make images of gods to worship, and we are not to use His name recklessly. Further, we are to remember who is the Creator, and we have an entire weekly system to remind us of it, for in six days He created and rested on the seventh. God is God, He is one God, and we are never to go out of those boundaries.

So I accept that Scripture teaches that we have one God and I also accept that Scripture teaches that the Father, Son, and Holy Spirit are one. We cannot understand that. How can we? We are limited in power, presence, and knowledge. We have limited capacity to accept anything outside the realm in which we live. But that is exactly the point. If we could understand God, would He be any different to us? Would He be God?

Let me tell you about my friend Sticky. Sticky was a simple yet wonderful creation. Sure, he was created with a smiling face, but on his own volition he had no ability to change his expression. He lived with his smiling face his whole life. In fact, this was not Sticky's only limitation (if you could call a smiling face a limitation). He had no ability for motion and no feeling. Sticky was two-dimensional, without volume. His life was to stay on the page on which he was drawn and continue to express the image that his creator had given him. As a two-dimensional stick man, Sticky had a similar yet different form than his creator, and an expression on his face that reflected something extra about his creator. One day, words appeared next to Sticky on the page. "This drawing makes me feel so happy I want to jump for joy." His creator felt happy and joyful, whatever that was, but it made his creator jump. Movement and feelings were things that Sticky had no concept of, but also what made him the creation and not the creator. He could simply accept that his creator was outside the realm of his own understanding, and indeed that was what made his creator so awesome in comparison.

It is how I answer the question for people asking me about the Trinity. If we were to examine what the Bible teaches about God, we would find much more about God that we couldn't truly fathom or understand. It is at this point that we know that there is much that can be confirmed in God's Word that He has graciously allowed us to understand, and that gives us a great confidence in having faith in God for the things we can't understand. God has unique attributes that make Him the Creator and us the creation. It is these uncommon attributes that show us God's stamp of authority recognized in His very character.

God is independent. He doesn't require instruction or teaching. Nobody is His counselor and nobody can add to Him knowledge or understanding that He doesn't already have. "Who has directed the Spirit of the LORD, or as His counselor has taught Him? With whom did He take counsel, and who instructed Him, and taught Him in the path of justice? Who taught Him knowledge, and showed Him the way of understanding?" (Isa. 40:13–14). This is something that simply is unrecognizable in any human.

God is unchanging. God remains constantly the same forever. "They will perish, but You will endure; yes, they will all grow old like a garment; like a cloak You will change them, and they will be changed. But You are the same, and Your years will have no end" (Ps. 102:26–27). I don't know about you but I have changed in so many ways, as has every human. I have changed in my ideas, changed in my physical looks; I have known nothing other than constant change. In fact, change is such a strong part of humanity that we are actually told to embrace it. It's like an if-you-can't-beat-it-join-it kind of thing.

God is infinite. " 'I am the Alpha and the Omega, the Beginning and the End,' says the Lord, 'who is and who was and who is to come, the Almighty' " (Rev. 1:8). This is where we can only bow our knees in our finite capacity as humans and say that while we cannot understand what it is to be infinite, we accept that our Creator is indeed so.

God is timeless. "Before the mountains were brought forth, or ever You had formed the earth and the world, even from everlasting to everlasting, You are God" (Ps. 90:2). The world truly can't handle this. How can someone be timeless? How can someone have no beginning? Therefore, with our limited human capacity we attempt to explain away the self-existent, timeless God with material process. Yet we still have a problem. As Henry Morris has explained:

Although it is impossible for us to comprehend fully this concept of an eternal, self-existing God, the only alternative is the concept of an eternal self-existent universe; and this concept is also incomprehensible. Eternal God or eternal matter — that is the choice.[1]

So we come to considering the authority of God in a "Trinitarian" sense, and as we do we must understand one thing: God is God. He is Father, He is the Son, and He is the Holy Spirit; He is one God. The way that we describe the Trinity is really simply the best we can do. We must accept the truth from Scripture when it talks of the deity of the Father, Son, and Holy Spirit, but our language will unfortunately fall short. Augustine recognized this and wrote:

When the question is asked: three what? Human language labors altogether under great poverty of speech. The answer, however, is given "three persons," not that it might be spoken but that it might not be left unspoken . . . in this Trinity two or three Persons are not any greater than one of them.[2]

If we want to accept the authority of God, we must first accept that only God can be a fit witness concerning Himself. Accepting the awesome truth of the Trinity and the authoritative aspects in the distinct roles of each of the three "Persons" of the godhead should amaze us and evoke a response of resounding active worship in our lives. Before we do so, however, we must make special consideration of one matter. All authority is attributed to our God, who is one God. We will certainly be looking at the different roles of the Son and the Spirit compared to that of the Father, but we will not be attributing more or less authority, for example, to Jesus or the Holy Spirit as to the Father.

---

1. Henry Morris, *The Genesis Record* (Grand Rapids, MI: Baker Books, 1997), p. 40.
2. Bruce Milne, *Know the Truth* (Downers Grove, IL: InterVarsity Press, 1998), p. 77.

The Bible shows us clearly that there are distinct roles within the oneness of the Trinity. Jesus our Savior, for example, came to earth and humbled Himself to become a man to accept the wrath of God over sin on His own shoulders. He did this in perfect submission to the Father as we saw Him pray, "not My will but Yours be done," in the Garden of Gethsemane, revealing Christ's humanity. Submission or distinction in role does not mean there is any lacking in authority. Jesus attributed to Himself equal authority with the Father and told us that all authority in heaven and earth had been given to Him (Matt. 28:18). What we do see, however, is distinct *examples* of God's authority working out uniquely in action through the Father, Son, and Holy Spirit.

Neither do we add Jesus' authority and the authority of the Holy Spirit and the Father to get the total authority of God. Deuteronomy 6:4 says, "Hear, O Israel: The LORD our God, the LORD is one!" Stuart Olyott explains it this way:

> You cannot have a collection of pieces that are less than God, put them together, and have God! He is not like a jigsaw. Nor is He like a human body, made up of many organs. You cannot add eternity and unchangeability and all power and holiness together, and make up God. He is not made up of parts. He is indivisible. He is one. All of Him is eternal. All of Him is unchangeable. All of Him is all-powerful. All of Him is holy. You cannot for instance take away His holiness, and leave most of God behind. If you could take away His holiness, you would have destroyed God for all that He is holy.[3]

HOW IS AUTHORITY DISPLAYED IN THE FATHER?

Even though this chapter is about the authority displayed in the Father, it is really important that we understand the Bible teaches that all of the divine character attributes discussed above

---

3. Stuart Olyott, *The Three Are One*, 3rd printing (Darlington, UK: Evangelical Press, 1996), p. 22–23.

are attributable to the Father, the Son, and the Holy Spirit. At this stage, we could say that there is plenty of ground for claiming the authority of the Father, looking at these attributes alone. What more is needed to stamp authority than to be timeless and unlimited in power, presence, and knowledge? Actually, it is in relation to the Father that we would have little argument about these attributes, even from Jehovah's Witnesses, Jews, or Muslims. As soon as the Bible teaches the divine character of the Son or the Holy Spirit, however, we soon part company with these folks.

It was in considering this chapter that I found my thoughts proceeding toward what it means to be the one true Father of all in a distinct recognition in comparison to what the Bible teaches of the Son or the Holy Spirit. If God is truly our Father, He is the true Dad of this world and we should see this message authentically shown in Scripture. Our earthly fathers are limited in their authority. My own earthly dad commanded respect and it was undoubted in my house that he was indeed the final say in all household matters. But in this chapter we are not talking about a father who has the limited authoritative capacity over his household. We are talking about the great Father of all. In fact, Scripture tells us that the whole idea of family (or fatherhood) has as its origin God the father. "For this reason I bow my knees to the Father of our Lord Jesus Christ, from whom the whole family in heaven and earth is named" (Eph. 3:14–15).

It is in this look at our heritage in God, the Father of all, that we can see authentic authority displayed in Him as our one true Father. This becomes particularly clear in God's relationship with the Israelites. While the Jews would regularly claim their authority through their heritage in Abraham, Isaac, and Israel, the Bible makes it perfectly clear that this lineage means nothing without the original fatherly authority of this universe. As we consider God our Father and His authority, let's also consider what authority we allow our earthly family heritage to have over our lives in comparison. In biblical history, we see that the Jews would often claim Abraham, their father, in justification for being right with God. While God blessed the whole world through the line of Abraham, eventually leading to our Savior, Jesus Christ, the Jews failed to recognize the forest for the trees. Let's now have a look at some passages that give us insight into the difference between the authority of our earthly fathers (or heritage) compared to acknowledging the ultimate authority and supreme fatherhood of God.

In Philippians 3 there is a special little section of Scripture where the Apostle Paul is giving an account of his heritage. In verses 5 and 6 we see a special and significant claim that Paul can uniquely make. *"Circumcised the eighth day, of the stock of Israel, of the tribe of Benjamin, a Hebrew of the Hebrews; concerning the law, a Pharisee; concerning zeal, persecuting the church; concerning the righteousness which is in the law, blameless."* It is a little like saying you are next in line for the throne. Paul's lineage was as good as it gets for a Jew, but Paul has something more to say about this lineage a few verses on. He states that he counts it as rubbish (even manure) compared to knowing Christ. To any Pharisee hearing this amazing statement from Paul, it would have been like he had disowned his own father. I can almost hear the rebuke: "Paul, Abraham is our great father; you are denying your lineage. How dare you!" To Paul, however, there was a significant difference. He was going from being Saul the Pharisee to Paul the Christian. Paul was claiming a new Father — the one who sent Christ as Savior and called Abraham in the first place.

In Matthew 3 we see John the Baptist preaching to the Pharisees and Sadducees. The legalistic Pharisees and the liberal Sadducees were normally in opposition to each other, but against Jesus they were united. The common ground they both had was in their claim of being God's chosen people through their father Abraham, Isaac, and Jacob (Israel). As they came together to hear John preach, John had this to say to them:

> Brood of vipers! Who warned you to flee from the wrath to come? Therefore bear fruits worthy of repentance,

and do not think to say to yourselves, "We have Abraham as our father." For I say to you that God is able to raise up children to Abraham from these stones (Matt. 3:7–9).

Normally, the Sadducees and Pharisees would not see any need to discuss repentance. They were Jews and believed they were safely tucked away as God's people through their father Abraham. Both had a complete misunderstanding of Scripture and heritage, and John the Baptist was reminding them of this fact. It is a little like someone saying that I am a Christian because my father was a Christian. Actually, so many people in today's society claim Christian roots through denominational lines because of family heritage. They claim a specific denomination because it is the family religion.

In 1995 my father died. He was at the time the great mentor in my life. My older brother Robert stepped in and took the baton from my dad, and then in 2002 the Lord took Robert home as well. It probably wasn't until then that I realized not only in head knowledge but also in the heart that my faith in God was truly a gift from God. It wasn't handed down by my family, whom I looked up to. Jesus was my Savior and it is God's hand that was on me. It was my Father in heaven who gave me the gift of faith.

John was trying to point this out to the Pharisees and the Sadducees. God has no grandchildren. You have no instant salvation through your father Abraham. Abraham has no authority to forgive your sins or to restore the pre-sin glory we once had in the Garden. Abraham is a man, and a dead one at that. But here is some authentic authority. God can raise His own children out of rocks. This is the great Father's authority. He has no subjection to lines of ancestry. Sure, those lines are important because it is through those lines that He promised the coming of His Son, but the heritage for our salvation is in Him, not Abraham. The line of Abraham shows us a significant detail about our Father in that He keeps the promise of His covenant with us.

Sometimes it takes an awful lot of instruction for people to get a message. Isaiah preached to Judah from around 740 to 686 B.C. He preached during a time that the kingdom was divided and Israel (particularly Judah) was not in a good place. They were given to empty ritualism and idolatry, and this had led them into a sinful and destructive lifestyle spiraling to the point of a heathen altar being set up in Solomon's temple. They were under constant harassment and siege from the Babylonian and Assyrian empires, and their condition both spiritually and as a nation had become desolate.

We have all heard the statement, "Pride comes before a fall." Israel, like the Pharisees and Sadducees John preached to, had become supercilious through a false sense of security in its heritage. Isaiah in this time pleads repentance on behalf of a nation. Who does he plead to? The Father; the one true Father.

ISAIAH 63:16–64:8

Verse 16: *Doubtless You are our Father, though Abraham was ignorant of us, and Israel does not acknowledge us. You, O LORD, are our Father; our Redeemer from Everlasting is Your name.*

Doubtless. Isaiah is bringing out his axiomatic presupposition. Whether Israel wants to believe it or not, it doesn't change the fact: God is our Father. He is from everlasting and He is our Redeemer. What a way to plead repentance: "Whether we have accepted it or not, You are our Father and we are wrong. It is we who need to turn and it is we who need to again accept You as our authority. We need to throw away the idols of our life and cast aside our pagan practices. We need to start recognizing You, God, as our Father."

Not only this, but Isaiah has beautifully captured the folly of a false heritage. Neither Abraham nor Jacob is getting Israel out of the mess. Neither Abraham nor Jacob can be their redeemer. Only the Father, who is undoubtedly their Father, has the authority to do so.

I am a huge supporter of the need for good, strong Christian dads in this world. Yet as one who has also been a child, I have to say that there have been many times in my life that I have paid more attention to my earthly dad than my Heavenly Father. Our parents are certainly stewards for our well-being and growth into adult-hood, but we must always remember that every course of action, statement, and thought in our life is first and foremost said and done under the headship of our Heavenly Father. We first answer to God whether we want to accept that or not, and if we don't accept it now, one day we will. The ultimate fatherhood authority for our life is our Father in heaven and no one else. Our earthly fathers, just like us, come under that authority, and there are grave consequences for rejecting the authority of our Heavenly Father. The consequences are far greater than anything we can dish out as earthly fathers.

Verse 17: *O LORD, why have you made us stray from Your ways, and hardened our heart from Your fear? Return for Your servants' sake, the tribes of Your inheritance.*

All through the Bible we get a great glimpse into man's heart. Genesis specifically shows us that sin has caused us great harm. We have no choice but evil. We reject God at every opportunity, and both before and after the great Flood of Noah, God saw that man's heart was only ever evil. Many in the modern Church don't like to preach this, but this is the biblical position on sin. We are com-pletely ruined in sin. Even the Apostle Paul refers to us all as being "dead" in our transgressions and sin. We are not weak or sick in sin, but dead. We need a miraculous, life-giving work to bring us back to life. It is only in this wonderful grace proceeding from the only one with the authority to give it that we have any ability at all to again please God in our life.

It is in understanding our position in sin that we can truly see the devastation of Israel's position. God has given them over to their sin. Even then, in His gracious and merciful faithfulness, He has kept a remnant among them, the likes of Isaiah who can plead on their behalf, and he certainly does. He pleads with God to again be their Father and not to take His preserving, providential presence from them.

So Isaiah is pleading with God to again look back at them. He is saying something like this: "Please look back at your people; please again have us rightfully acknowledge our inheritance is only in you. Once more have us accept that you are the authority in this world and not us." This is the pleading of Isaiah.

While we are specifically thinking of the Father in this chapter, this verse of pleading caused me to remember the wonderful words of a hymn written around A.D. 375, saying much the same thing to Jesus. This is the same sort of prayer that Isaiah was praying to the Father when he said, "Return for your servants' sake."

Lord Jesus, think on me and purge away my sin;
From earthborn passions set me free and make me pure within.
Lord Jesus, think on me amid the battle's strife;
In all my pain and misery be thou my health and life.
Lord Jesus, think on me nor let me go astray;
Through darkness and perplexity point thou the heavenly way.[4]

This depicts Isaiah's prayer beautifully. Israel had rejected the Father's great authority for a misdirected confidence in Abraham and Jacob, but that had let them down. As a result, they were then left to wallow in a spiral of sinful destruction, but Isaiah pleads: Father, think on us.

Verse 18: *Your holy people have possessed it but a little while; our adversaries have trodden down Your sanctuary.*

If we could only step out of our own skin every now and then and have a look at our life in the light of this life of Israel. Israel had rejected the Father's authority, and in like manner, our rejection of the Father's authority not only leads us personally to sinful desolation, but the world and Satan's kingdom stamps *its* authority on our life. A modern example of this is the sad story of Charles Templeton.

---

4. "Lord Jesus, Think on Me," written by Synesius of Cyrene, translated by Allen W. Chatfield.

In the 1950s Charles Templeton was voted as one of the "best used by God" for the evangelical movement of the time. He was a prominent evangelist and for a time surpassed even a young Billy Graham. But written records of his discussions with Billy Graham show Charles Templeton had been rejecting God's authority in Genesis in favor of fallible human belief systems. Rather than looking at the evidence through a biblical bias, Templeton fell for the anti-God neutral approach to this physical world, and soon found himself questioning every portion of Scripture, including the death and Resurrection of Jesus Christ. Templeton was given over to the theories of this world, and eventually Satan's kingdom stamped authority on Templeton's life. Sadly, he died an atheist.

Charles Templeton never really accepted the Father's authority. He lived among people who did and even taught the gospel through which many came to salvation in the Lord Jesus. Sadly, as Charles spiraled further and further into the acceptance of man's authority over God's, he became not only removed from his Christian roots and thinking, but he became part of the mainstream rejection of God that we see in the world. This may sound somewhat crass, yet in all respects, Charles Templeton showed himself as just another pagan.

Verse 19: *We have become like those of old, over whom You never ruled, those who were never called by Your name.*

This is exactly what had happened to Israel. In verse 19 Isaiah recounts to God that Israel may have lived in God's holy promised land, but they had become just like every other nation about them. Do we realize fully that the rejection of any aspect of the Father's authority is just simply dangerous?

Every time I hear the Charles Templeton story, it saddens me. It really does. When you can see so clearly how a presupposition of God's authority, biblical authority, makes so much sense of the physical world around us, you just become saddened by anyone who wants to compromise that. For Charles Templeton, it wasn't just origins. His position of allowing man's fallible interpretation of evidence to infiltrate God's authoritative Word consistently flowed in that manner through to a denial of the gospel and Jesus Christ. In one sense you might think it is wrong for me to feel like I just want to go back in time and grab Charles and shake him as hard as I can until he comes to his senses. *"What are you thinking, dude?!"* Yes, that's a bit physical, but metaphorically that is what I wish I could do, and this is how Isaiah now prays. He asks the Father to shake some sense into Israel that they might again see who truly is their God, their authority, and their one true Father:

> 64:1–5a: *Oh, that You would rend the heavens! That You would come down! That the mountains might shake at Your presence — as fire burns brushwood, as fire causes water to boil — to make Your name known to Your adversaries, that the nations may tremble at Your presence! When You did awesome things for which we did not look, You came down, the mountains shook at your presence. For since the beginning of the world men have not heard nor perceived by the ear, nor has the eye seen any God besides You, who acts for the one who waits for Him. You meet him who rejoices and does righteousness, who remembers You in Your ways.*

If you have a Father who has ultimate authority over all there is because He is the self-existent, timeless Creator, it would be an entirely appropriate response to spread His fame as far and wide as you possibly can. God had chosen Israel as His people, to be His light and to show His magnificent fame like a national mission to the world. Isaiah is praying for the Lord to return and shake things up that Israel might again remember God, the sovereign and authoritative Father of their fathers.

> Verse 5b–7: *You are indeed angry, for we have sinned — in these ways we continue; and we need to be saved. But we are all like an unclean thing, and all our righteousnesses are*

like filthy rags; we all fade as a leaf, and our iniquities, like the
wind, have taken us away. And there is no one who calls on
Your name, who stirs himself up to take hold of You; for You
have hidden Your face from us, and have consumed us because
of our iniquities.

Every sincere Christian has faced the anguish of his or her sin-
fulness as expressed in this verse. God is angry at sin and He has
every right to be. He is the author of life and as such expects obedience. In an outpouring of His glory and love He created us in His
own image. We are the image of our Father and our response is to
reject Him. We don't even call on His name. And so Isaiah prays this
prayer for us. We should pray it as well — *God, enable us to seek Your*
face. We need Your enabling to even seek You, and we realize that any
goodness we claim for ourselves is so flimsy that it gets blown away by
the wind. It is so important that we see the wonderful and fearsome
truth of this verse. *We answer to our Father* whether we want to or
not. The Father's authority is such that He is ultimately the one we
answer to for our entire life.

God is angry at our sin, and one day we will stand before Him
to give account. On that day it will only be our self-denying acceptance of Jesus Christ that will make any difference. What I love
most about these verses is that Isaiah is asking a deep soul-searching
question: "Who stirs himself up to take hold of You?" It is when we
stop pointing the finger at Israel and saying what a terrible people
they are and look truly into the mirror of our lives that we can ask
this question. This message is for us, not just Israel, and on our
behalf Isaiah asks it of our Father in heaven, who has unquestionable
authority. "Who stirs himself up to take hold of You?" It becomes
time to open the dark closet and look deep within. Are there any of
man's fallible theories in your closet that have usurped the authority
of the Father? Are there practices that are unbecoming to His glory?
Are there idols that take the place of Him in worship in your every-
day life? How full is that closet? So stir yourself up, ask God to shake

the mountains of your life, and succumb to His authority and seek His face. The face of our Father. The face of authority.

Verse 8: *But now, O LORD, You are our Father; we are the clay, and You our potter; and all we are the work of Your hand.*

As we stop at this verse in the passage, Isaiah has made it clear. We are the Father's pottery. Israel was God's chosen people. They were to be the wonderful centerpiece in the middle of the table, the glory of the potter. In fact, this is exactly how Adam and Eve were in the perfect creation. How could they be anything less than the standout piece of creation in bearing the image of their Maker? In the devastation of sin we have all become broken pottery, and it is only through the mercy and grace of the Father that we can again show His image and become useful. Praise God that in His mercy some are saved for His eternal glory and the glory of His awesome Son.

And this is the final call of the Lord. *"Does not the potter have power over the clay, from the same lump to make one vessel for honor and another for dishonor?"* (Rom. 9:21). Which piece of pottery are you? Are you the honorable centerpiece reflecting the glory and respecting the authority of the Potter, or are you rejecting the Potter's authority and being used as a scrap dish? This may sound harsh in some respects, so it is important that I qualify. I am not telling you that you are worthless. In sin, we, including me, are *all* worthless. Sin has utterly destroyed any worth we previously had. From conception we are the Potter's scrap dish because we are sinful from conception. But God, through Jesus Christ and His sacrifice for us on the Cross, can mold us into a creation of His glory, and He makes in us a worth more valuable than the most precious jewels, because it is the worth of Christ in us. We become won for the Father through Christ who has won us. We become molded in the hands of the only one who has authority to make us into a wonderful reflection of Himself, and we are made more and more beautiful in Him as He transforms us into His wonderful image.

Through Christ, our Father values us as being worth more than anything in His creation, and we become the centerpiece of the Potter's handiwork.

God the Father is the Potter. He is the authority, not us. We are the clay. The Father has authentic authority because He truly is the Father, the Creator. He has authority because just removing His sustaining power from our lives leaves us in deep desolation. His authority is proven in His sovereign grace in salvation. His authority is without question because He is "doubtless" our Father above any human heritage. His authority is authentic as He is the potter who molds us into His image and no one else's. He is the authority, because He simply IS. The Father's authority matters, and it matters a great deal.

O God, Thou art the Father of all that have believed;
From whom all hosts of angels have life and power received.
O God, Thou art the Maker of all created things,
The righteous Judge of judges, the almighty King of kings.

High in the heavenly Zion thou reignest God adored;
And in the coming glory thou shalt be sovereign Lord.
Beyond our ken Thou shinest, the everlasting Light;
Ineffable in loving, unthinkable in might.

Thou to the meek and lowly thy secrets dost unfold;
O God, Thou doest all things, all things both new and old.
I walk secure and blessèd in every clime or coast,
In name of God the Father, and Son, and Holy Ghost.[5]

---

5. "O God, Thou Art the Father," words by Columba (521–597), translated by Duncan MacGregor.

Chapter 7

Authority and God the Son

I AM WHO I AM.
— God (Exod. 3:14)

I was sitting in my church listening to our pastor Jens (pronounced Yens) as he preached through Malachi. Jens came to a point that made me think more about how I view Jesus when he made a comment about "the storybook Jesus."

Have you ever seen Jesus in the storybooks? Maybe it is in your children's Bible or children's devotional material. It's pretty easy to describe the pictures of Jesus in these books. He has long, black, flowing hair, surrounded by a group of young children, some of whom may be holding on to His tunic. The children around Him look happy, content, and playful, and Jesus is holding a little lamb in His arms. It is the classic picture of Jesus, isn't it? The storybook Jesus.

Jens made me start thinking of the Jesus I most often think about. It really is a question worth asking. When you think of Jesus, who is the Jesus you are thinking of? In one sense it is a stupid question because Jesus is who He is regardless of what we perceive. I suppose I am asking us all to question our perception against Scripture. We worship the God of Scripture, the Jesus of Scripture; and we are called to do so in spirit and in truth.

So after many Sundays preaching through Malachi, Jens came to chapter 3 where Malachi foretells the coming of Jesus:

> "Behold, He is coming," says the LORD of hosts. But who can endure the day of His coming? And who can stand when He appears? For He is like a refiner's fire and like launderers' soap. He will sit as a refiner and a purifier of silver; He will purify the sons of Levi, and purge them as gold and silver, that they may offer to the LORD an offering in righteousness (Mal. 3:1–3).

Is this the storybook Jesus? Well, no. This is Jesus. This is the biblical Jesus who comes in full authority and whom no one can endure. His power and authority are matchless. He takes us and refines us of impurity. He is the same Jesus that John writes of in Revelation 19:11–16. This is the Jesus who is the King of kings and Lord of lords. He is the one who judges and whose eyes are like a flame of fire and who is crowned with many crowns. He is the Jesus who is to come and will be followed by the armies of heaven. From His mouth comes a sharp sword and with it He will strike the nations. He brings the fierceness of the wrath of God.

Perhaps we should get our children's Bible illustrators to draw that Jesus as well as the Jesus holding the lamb, letting the little children come unto Him. The biblical Jesus is the authoritative reigning Jesus. The God of all there is. It is no surprise, therefore, that when the Apostle John is given a vision of Jesus, he sees Jesus coming in the final judgment of this world as a reigning King with a host of heavenly army following behind. He is truly the all-conquering, reigning Jesus of justice and the King of kings and the Lord of lords.

If we want to consider authority in relation to Jesus, the first thing we must do is adapt our own perceptions of Jesus to the actual scriptural account of who He is. We cannot in any manner dismiss that Jesus is the compassionate one, serving us, humbling Himself, healing others, weeping over His friends, and crying out for the city of Jerusalem. He is the Jesus who also taught us about love and brought people from the most opposite of spectrums and made them His Apostles, building His team in complete unity. His objective on the Cross was mercy and overwhelming, all-abounding grace. Yet the Bible clearly shows that we also cannot dismiss that Jesus did all He did with full and eternal authority that can only come with true deity and kingship. Sadly, some came in direct contact with Christ and heard His teaching and witnessed His miracles and still rejected His authority for their own fallible human kingship. Maybe their perception was just that of the loving, healing, "good man" Jesus, and not of the authoritative Lord.

In John's gospel we are made aware that it was foretold that people would reject Christ and His authority even after having seen His marvelous works:

> But although He had done so many signs before them, they did not believe in Him, that the word of Isaiah the prophet might be fulfilled, which he spoke: "Lord, who has believed our report? And to whom has the arm of the LORD been revealed?" Therefore they could not believe, because Isaiah said again: "He has blinded their eyes and hardened their hearts, lest they should see with their eyes, lest they should understand with their hearts and turn, so that I should heal them" (John 12:37–40).

In this passage, John quoted from Isaiah 53:1 and 6:10 to show that it was expected that people would deny Christ's divine authority. In fact, John points out that this prophecy concerning people's rejection of Christ came to Isaiah from God when Isaiah had seen His glory firsthand. It is on this subject of those rejecting the deity of Jesus Christ and the authoritative kingship of Christ that verse 40 of John 12 becomes a significant verse. Concerning Jesus, John says, *"These things Isaiah said when he saw His glory and spoke of Him."*

Isaiah wrote this more than 700 years before Jesus walked among us, so what could he have possibly seen?

If we go back to John's quoted passage from Isaiah 6:10 and read from the beginning of the chapter, we find an account of the vision Isaiah saw:

> In the year that King Uzziah died, I saw the Lord sitting on a throne, high and lifted up, and the train of His robe filled the temple. Above it stood seraphim; each one had six wings: with two he covered his face, with two he covered his feet, and with two he flew. And one cried to another and said: "Holy, holy, holy is the LORD of hosts; the whole earth is full of His glory!" (Isa. 6:1–3).

If you are not amazed yet, let me point it out to you. John tells us that Isaiah's vision was of Jesus Christ. Isaiah, at an appointed time (in the year of King Uzziah's death) around 700 years earlier than the arrival of Jesus on earth, was given a glimpse of the throne room of heaven and saw the reigning pre-incarnate Christ. It was such a powerful thing for Isaiah to see that he instantly bowed his knees and repented of the sin and impurity of his life. We could stop this chapter right now having ascertained Christ's authority. Before Jesus came to earth, He was already King. He has always been King and will always be King. What more authority do we need to establish? The whole earth is full of His glory and His holiness. *"Holy, holy, holy is the Lord God Almighty, the whole earth is full of His glory!"*

Jesus' authority is clearly authenticated in that He is eternally God and Creator. Isaiah witnessed Jesus' authority on the throne with all power and dominion prior to the incarnation, and John clearly (led by the Holy Spirit) knew that to be the case. John, also in the beginning of his gospel account, points to the eternal deity (and thus authority) of Jesus. Most Christians know the passage from John 1 well: *"In the beginning was the Word, and the Word was with God, and the Word was God. He was in the beginning with*

God" (John 1:1–2). John, here talking of Jesus, attributes to Him an eternal nature and both a presence with God and actually being God. This certainly can only be understood to any degree in an acceptance of the doctrine of the Trinity, but that is not our point for this book. Further in John 1, also attributed to the Word is light, life, all of creation, the incarnation, the glory of the Father, and the fullness of grace and truth.

The entire Scriptures, both Old and New Testaments, attribute to Christ an authentic authority that can only be found in one who is truly God, and the Scriptures are actually very careful in pointing that out consistently. Many in this world, such as the Jehovah's Witnesses, do not wish to accept the fullness of Christ's authority and therefore primarily reject His deity. This is where it is good for us to consider such a passage of Scripture as the opening verses of John's gospel, and see the strongest degree of care in the explanation of who Jesus really is, as the Eternal One, unmade, never created but always existing. As Stuart Olyott explains:

> John says that this eternal Unmade was eternally with God. But this does not mean that He was less than God, as the Semi-Arians contend. The Word was God. John is as dogmatic as that about the deity of Christ, and his words stand as a perpetual contradiction of the Semi-Arian position. There is no way to dismiss these words, or to evade their full impact. Indeed, the way in which John arranges his words in the original Greek (with the predicate preceding the subject) means that he is actually stressing the full deity of Christ. It would be perfectly legitimate to render his words "and the Word was God himself."[1]

Actually, it is very difficult to read any account of Jesus and not see an amazing godly authority. We can just think of any of His miracles showing that He had authority over the physical things of

---

1. Stuart Olyott, *Jesus Is Both God and Man* (Darlington, UK: Evangelical Press, 2000), p. 23.

this world. The winds and waves obeyed Him. When no earthly physician could heal them, the lame could walk and the blind could see. Jesus showed authority over life and death and raised His friend Lazarus to life and conquered death Himself. He was teaching the priests Scriptures by the age of 12 (according to Luke 2:42), indicating that they are indeed *His* Word. Not only this, but attributed to Christ throughout the New Testament is the name "Lord" (*Kyrios* — the Greek version of Jehovah).

We have been considering in this book if authority matters and whether we want to accept it or not. The claim of Scripture is that Christ is indeed the authority and that the Word of God comes from Him. Anyone pursuing knowledge or wisdom should first understand that Christ is the originator and authority over all revealed knowledge and wisdom because He is the eternally existent Creator God without whom there would be nothing (Col. 2:3). When Paul was writing to the Corinthians, in his first letter to them he introduced the letter by thanking God that they had been truly open to knowledge through Jesus Christ:

> I thank my God always concerning you for the grace of God which was given to you by Christ Jesus, that you were enriched in everything by Him in all utterance and all knowledge, even as the testimony of Christ was confirmed in you, so that you come short in no gift, eagerly waiting for the revelation of our Lord Jesus Christ (1 Cor. 1:4–7).

In this passage, Paul points out to the Corinthians that in Christ and from conversion they are on the road of speaking from an authoritative base of knowledge, because Christ is the originator of knowledge and wisdom. Paul's first remarks of thanks to God are for this. In Christ we commence our walk in the light, but we should be constantly reminded that our utterances (speech or teaching) and knowledge are only rich and true when they are in Christ. It is why Paul says that this is what happens when the testimony of Christ is confirmed in us (conversion). Through repentance and faith we have rejected the principles of fallible human reason for the authoritative presupposition that Christ is the foundation of knowledge and wisdom. We therefore should both think in Christ and speak in Christ, and this means that His Word from Genesis to Revelation must be the foundation and first point of all that we speak and think.

Paul consistently comes back to this point in his letters — that all knowledge and wisdom is in Christ, and that this world is shown to be foolish in comparison. Take for example the following verses from Colossians:

> For this reason we also, since the day we heard it, do not cease to pray for you, and to ask that you may be filled with the knowledge of His will in all wisdom and spiritual understanding; that you may walk worthy of the Lord, fully pleasing Him, being fruitful in every good work and increasing in the knowledge of God (Col. 1:9–10).

> Beware lest anyone cheat you through philosophy and empty deceit, according to the tradition of men, according to the basic principles of the world, and not according to Christ. For in Him dwells all the fullness of the Godhead bodily; and you are complete in Him, who is the head of all principality and power (Col. 2:8–10).

> In whom are hidden all the treasures of wisdom and knowledge (Col. 2:3).

When speaking of Jesus, Paul is very clear. He teaches us from his Christ-appointed, apostolic authority that Jesus is our wisdom and knowledge, and that we are to be very careful not to allow the empty deceit of this world to infiltrate the perfect wisdom and knowledge of God. Unfortunately, there are many, including revered academics, who have compromised Christ's authority in knowledge and wisdom by interpreting His Word through worldly philosophy rather than considering the worldly philosophy through His Word.

Paul's teaching would have us think upon the domain of Christ's authority. Jesus is the foundation for ALL wisdom and knowledge. We respect Christ when we authentically preach His gospel and the truth of His ministry and work on the Cross. But when we reject the authority of the Bible in any other area, we reject the authority of this same Christ of the Cross. Many people have said to me that it doesn't matter whether we get Genesis right or not as long as we respect Jesus' teaching and work on the Cross. We so often forget that Genesis *is* Jesus' teaching, and this is the most common error of the rejection of the authority of His Word today.

We come here to the crux of accepting Christ's authority. The Church is so willing to speak of Christ's love and to accept that Christ has the authority to forgive sin, to die, and to conquer death, to equip and empower His Church, and to return in judgment on the final consummation of creation. I have had wonderful experiences coming under the teaching of many good men holding true to the teachings of Christ, especially in matters of the gospel. In saying that, a clear point needs to be made by every teacher: the same Christ of the gospel is the Christ of creation. Christ's authority is His authorship of the entire Word of God. Christ's words are not just the ones written in red ink in some Bibles but the entire Word of God. The domain of Christological teaching has His gospel at the center but is founded in the authority of His entire Word, and when we reject His authority in other parts of His Word, we compromise His central message. It is the authority of Jesus Christ that trumps the claims of authority made by every secular scientist or philosopher or expert in any field. Upholding the authority of Jesus Christ is not just upholding the message of the Cross. It is upholding the authority of His entire Word from the very first verse.

It is time the Church started to uphold the authority of our Savior the way in which He has instructed us to uphold it in His Word. Paul makes it clear that as Christians we should not allow the philosophies of this world to cheat us. The matter of origins is the battleground today where we are compromising Christ's authority, and it *is* Christ's authoritative domain. There are many who will not be comfortable with me saying it this way. It is not only biblical authority that we are compromising when we interpret Genesis through the eyes of the world's philosophies and presuppositions concerning evidence. We are compromising Christ's authority, and this is the authority that extends to and impacts the message of His gospel.

We need to think seriously about this, and we need to be consistent in the application of Scripture across the board. We cannot be consistent and accept the authority of Christ in regard to His work on the Cross and His miracles and His gospel grace unless we are also prepared to accept His kingship and authority in knowledge and wisdom in the entirety of His Word.

When I see my brothers around me compromising Christ's authority in any area of doctrine, I feel sincerely sad. I certainly unite with them in Christ and the gospel, but I also cannot support their stand on allowing human philosophy to shape their Scripture focus. The world has also seen this contradiction, and many deem the Church irrelevant as a result.

I also strongly believe that in our attempt to be academic we can sometimes be too smart for ourselves. Some of our academic brethren have seen the matter of origins as a scientific one, while others have seen it as a theological one. While there are truths in both of these, the matter of origins is a matter of history, God's history. The theological perspectives we obtain from that history are certainly rich, and science certainly can be used to confirm that history, as we have shown in previous chapters. But we must always understand that Christ is the authority when it comes to history, science, or theology, for He is the authority on all matters of knowledge and wisdom. This covers every field of thought.

In the most practical and amazing way, Christ has truly proven His authority over history. "All we like sheep have gone astray; we have turned, every one, to his own way; and the LORD has laid on Him the iniquity of us all. He was oppressed and He was afflicted, yet He opened not His mouth; He was led as a lamb to the slaughter, and as a sheep that before its shearers is silent, so He opened not his mouth" (Isa. 53:6–7). Isaiah, over 700 years in advance, was given this prophetic Word from God to share with Israel. In fact, Isaiah's prophecies throughout his book give us the whole gospel work of Jesus in great detail. Jesus in this way has been in complete authority over history as He came into this earth and fulfilled what He told us He would do through Isaiah 700 years earlier.

Whether we accept it or not, Christ is the authority and the authority over all. In the last verse in the gospel of Matthew we read that Christ (in His appearing after the Resurrection) commissioned us to spread His gospel in full authority. In fact, He explains that all authority in heaven and earth has been given to Him. It is with this authority that we go out to the world with the message of His good news. When we compromise the authority that sends us, we compromise the strength of the message we go with. All authority in heaven and earth is Christ's. He is our Savior and Lord and commissions us in authority to take His fame to the ends of the world. It is not up to us to question that authority but to submit to our Lord in accepting His Word and preaching it in its entirety to a lost world.

We are therefore left with a decision to make. Will we truly accept Christ's authority? That means that one cannot accept just part of Christ's authority, for then it would not be an authority. Either Christ is truly the authority or He is a counterfeit authority. His Word does not allow for us to consider Christ's authority in part. His Word remains consistent with Christ having authentic and full authority.

If anyone were going to deny Christ's genuine authority, it would have been His own family. I know my mother loves me and thinks much of me, but there is no way my mum would consider me to be divine. There is no way my mum would worship me. She knows me too well. She has seen my sin and all my blemishes. She has seen me make unwise decisions and do things that people should not follow. I am a counterfeit authority. The closest people in our lives know our faults and sins better than any other humans. Yet, in Acts 1:14, within the first list of those associated with worshiping Christ as His Church are Mary, His mother, and His brothers. They were convinced of Jesus' authority when they knew Him and His past on earth better than anyone. Nobody would have convinced them otherwise. They came under His authority. Why? Because they learned Jesus' authority is without question. The Scriptures confirm it, and the evidence confirms the historical accuracy of the Scriptures that confirm it. Yet regardless of confirmation, Jesus' authority simply is.

So on this note I must ask this question: do you accept Jesus' authority in full or part? Please answer truthfully.

Finally, we cannot discuss Jesus' authority without discussing His authority displayed through His work on the Cross. But we also must certainly understand the biblical account that the incarnate Christ is not only fully God in deity but fully human.

Prior to Jesus being brought to trial, we see Jesus praying in the Garden of Gethsemane that God might take His cup of wrath from Him. The humanity of Jesus is clearly displayed in this prayer. He knew what He was to do for the sake of reconciling His creation, but the task was overwhelming. He was to come under the fearsome judgment of the Father's wrath on sin as a sinless sacrifice.

The Father's wrath on sin is an overwhelming anger that we really have no concept of. In the Garden of Eden (and ever since) we have rejected His eternal and divine kingship to desire our own rule: self rule. As a holy, righteous, perfect, omnipotent Creator, His anger at this is hard for us to imagine — anger that is perfect and justifiably righteous in every way. Jesus was about to take on that wrath for us in perfect submission to the will of His Father. So terrible is this prospect that Jesus sweats blood as He prays to the Father in preparation for an act that He had determined before the creation of the world. In *The Murder of Jesus*, John MacArthur gives some insight into this pain that Christ was suffering:

It was no hyperbole when Jesus told the disciples that His distress was so severe that it had brought Him to the very brink of death. The agony He bore in the garden was literally sufficient to kill Him — and may well have done so if God were not preserving Him for another means of death. Luke records that "His sweat became like great drops of blood falling down to the ground" (Luke 22:44). That describes a rare but well-documented malady known as "hematidrosis" that sometimes occurs under heavy emotional distress. Subcutaneous capillaries burst under stress and the blood mingles with one's perspiration, exiting through the sweat glands.[2]

Jesus goes through the torment of betrayal, capture, corrupt judgments, denial by His disciple Peter, floggings, beatings, and then being nailed to a Cross. Then comes the reason Christ was sweating blood. "And about the ninth hour Jesus cried out with a loud voice, saying, 'Eli, Eli, lama sabachthani?' That is, 'My God, My God, why have You forsaken Me?' " (Matt. 27:46). The lyrics of the Stuart Townend song put it this way: "How great the pain of searing loss, The Father turns His face away, As wounds which mar the chosen One, Bring many sons to glory."[3]

Prior to that point and knowing it was coming, Jesus heard the crowd yelling at Him. " 'If You are the Son of God, come down from the cross.' Likewise the chief priests also, mocking with the scribes and elders, said, 'He saved others; Himself He cannot save. If He is the King of Israel, let Him now come down from the cross, and we will believe Him. He trusted in God; let Him deliver Him now if He will have Him; for He said, "I am the Son of God" ' " (Matt. 27:40–43).

Prove yourself! We have heard it all before, haven't we? The fact is, Jesus was proving Himself and authenticating His godly authority. He was fulfilling His authority over history, over sin, over death,

---

2. John MacArthur, *The Murder of Jesus* (Nashville, TN: Thomas Nelson Publishers, 2004), p. 68.
3. "How Deep the Father's Love for Us," www.ap0s7le.com/list/song/28/Stuart_Townend/How_Deep_The_Father's_Love_For_Us/

over humanity. Jesus was also proving His authority by not giving in to those standing around Him claiming their authority over Him. Neither the priests, nor Pilate, nor the Romans were in authority over Jesus. They might have thought they were, but they were all subject to His authoritative plan of salvation. We might want to think the Jews put Jesus on the Cross or even that we put Jesus on the Cross, but Scripture tells us differently. Second Timothy 1:9 records that God *"has saved us and called us with a holy calling, not according to our works, but according to His own purpose and grace which was given to us in Christ Jesus before time began."*

Those surrounding Christ at the foot of the Cross may have wanted Christ to prove His authority by calling down angels or miraculously coming down from the Cross, but Christ's authority was being proven in His power to fulfill His redemptive history.

In the last chapter, we saw what happens to us when the Father removes His providential presence from our lives. Isaiah showed us (as one example of many in Scripture) that we become desolate and hopeless in our own sin and unable to even seek God unless He returns His favor. But we see something uniquely different in Christ. The Father turns His face as wounds mar the chosen One. The chosen One becomes sin for us (2 Cor. 5:21), dies, and three days later rises in glorious victory over death. Christ has taken the awful brunt of the Father's turned face but now reigns with the Father in heaven. We can never know the extent of Christ's anguish to which the Father forsakes the Son as Jesus yelled out that question: "Why have You forsaken Me?" The justice and wrath poured down on Christ in substitution for us are something we can never know, but this is the authority Christ has over death and sin that He now reigns with the Father after taking the full brunt of His wrath for us (Heb 1:13).

So let us bow before the Lord of all. Let us not reduce His authority where we want to. The Lord over death and sin is the Lord of creation and history. He is the Lord of His Word revealed to us in full authority. It is in this unlimited authority that Christ appeared

again to His disciples and told them to go out and make disciples
of all men, baptizing them in the name of the Father and of the Son
and of the Holy Spirit.

> Who is this so weak and helpless,
> Child of lowly Hebrew maid,
> Rudely in a stable sheltered, coldly in a manger laid?
> 'Tis the Lord of all creation,
>   who this wondrous path hath trod;
> He is God from everlasting, and to everlasting God.
>
> Who is this, a Man of sorrows, walking sadly life's hard way,
> Homeless, weary, sighing, weeping, over sin and Satan's sway?
> 'Tis our God, our glorious Savior, who above the starry sky
> Now for us a place prepareth, where no tear can dim the eye.
>
> Who is this? Behold Him shedding drops of blood upon the
>   ground!
> Who is this, despised, rejected, mocked, insulted, beaten, bound?
> 'Tis our God, who gifts and graces on His church now
>   poureth down;
> Who shall smite in righteous judgment all His foes
>   beneath His throne.
>
> Who is this that hangeth dying
>   while the rude world scoffs and scorns,
> Numbered with the malefactors, torn with nails,
>   and crowned with thorns?
> 'Tis the God who ever liveth, 'mid the shining ones on high,
> In the glorious golden city, reigning everlastingly.[4]

Does the authority of the Son matter? I think you will find it
does.

---

4. "Who Is This So Weak and Dying?" www.cyberhymnal.org/htm/w/h/o/
whoisthi.htm.

Chapter 8

Authority and God the Holy Spirit

I AM WHO I AM.
— God (Exod. 3:14)

We are going to discuss how authority is shown in the working of the Holy Spirit, but you will have to humor me for a couple of pages.

"For like some others, you are under the delusion that our God is a donkey's head."[1] Tertullian was one of our early church fathers, born around A.D. 150, and he wrote this in response to the Christian critics of his time. It was a widely spread rumor that was reported to have originated with a Roman senator and historian, Cornelius Tacitus. The idea was that the Jews took guidance from thirsty donkeys in the desert after escaping from Egypt. Tacitus believed that the donkeys led the Jews to water and as a result they had commenced worshiping the image of a donkey's head. He believed the Christians to be closely associated with the Jews and claimed that they too worshiped the head of a donkey, but also

1. www.logoslibrary.org/tertullian/apology/16.html.

associated that to Christ. Tertullian wrote in the 16th chapter of his *Apology* a strong defense of this outrageous claim and in fact pointed out much hypocrisy in Tacitus' claims. One major point Tertullian makes is that in the demolishing of the temple in A.D. 70 there was not one image within the temple that represented any animal at all. Surely if there was worship to an image of a donkey from the Jews, it would be present in the temple where Jewish worship occurred.

Tertullian was in actuality a fairly significant Church father. Bruce Shelly's book *Church History in Plain Language* states the following about Tertullian:

> Tertullian's *Apology* underlined the legal and moral absurdity of the persecution directed against Christians. Some of his other books offered encouragement to those facing martyrdom. He attacked the heretics, explained the Lord's Prayer and the meaning of baptism, and helped develop the orthodox understanding of the Trinity. He was the first person to use the Latin word "trinitas" (trinity). . . . His intellectual brilliance and literary versatility made him one of the most powerful writers of the time.[2]

Tertullian was also one of the Christian fathers who recognized the use of the Cross as a symbol for Christians.

In 1857, after the unearthing of a building in Palatine Hill in Rome, graffiti was found engraved on one of its walls mocking the Christian worship of Christ. The graffiti has become known as the "Alexamenos Graffito." It has been dated by archaeologists to be perpetrated around the same time (or a little after) Tertullian. Basically, the graffiti depicts Christ on the Cross. However, instead of a human head He has the head of a donkey. There is a man at the foot of the Cross who looks to be in prayer. The caption on the drawing is translated "Alexamenos worships (his) God." It is interesting when we look at this to gain some perspective of the age in which

---

2. Bruce Shelly, *Church History in Plain Language* (Dallas, TX: Word Publishing, 1995), p. 34.

Tertullian and perhaps also our graffiti artist was living. It is certainly plain that there was widespread persecution of the Church, and in fact to be a Christian at that time in Rome was illegal. There were misconceptions about the Church and what it believed, but those misconceptions came from one overruling attitude. Christianity to the world was foolishness. If you asked the Apostle Paul, he would tell you that even in Tertullian's time this was not new.

Tracing of the "Alexamenos Graffito"
(Source: www.commons.wikimedia.org)

Today, 1,800 years later, I find no difference as I look around the world we live in. To many, Christianity remains foolishness, the Bible remains foolishness, Christ remains foolishness, belief in God remains foolishness, and the world doesn't mind telling us. You don't have to watch television long to hear some cheap shot at Christians, especially on comedy shows. The ideas of today and Tertullian's time (and the time of the Apostles) are really no different. Today the world might prefer to use creatures such as unicorns rather than donkeys, but the theory is still the same. As an example, Clarence Darrow (the famous defense attorney in the Scopes trial of 1925) held the following view: "*I don't believe in God because I don't believe in Mother Goose.*"[3] Many people think we are donkeys worshiping a donkey (or in Darrow's words, a goose). Unfortunately, part of that reason is because Christians have not equipped themselves in defending the Scriptures from secular reasoning. We are generally not standing on

---
3. en.wikiquote.org/wiki/Clarence_Darrow.

the authority of the Word of God to understand the evidence in this world. We have overwhelming evidence that confirms the history and thus authority of the Bible, and a good majority of us have remained ignorant of our defenses and allowed the world to mock God as a donkey (or a goose).

Dr. Dawkins constantly refers to Christians as people who have no substance for what they believe and uses this to mock God in the same way as Darrow and the people of Tertullian's time. He writes:

> A popular deity on the Internet at present — and as undisprovable as Yahweh or any other — is the Flying Spaghetti Monster, who many claim has touched them with his noodly appendage. I am delighted to see that the Gospel of the Flying Spaghetti Monster has now been published as a book, to great acclaim. I haven't read it myself, but who needs to read a gospel when you just know it's true?[4]

Are we really that stupid? Dr. Dawkins is basically saying that we have a blind faith and if you have a blind faith you may as well believe in the tooth fairy or the spaghetti monster. Perhaps if Dr. Dawkins was the perpetrator of the graffiti it might simply have a bowl of spaghetti instead of the head of a donkey. There is no difference.

What Dr. Dawkins is not saying is that he has already seen a lot of strong evidence in favor of the Bible and denied it. Just by reading through his book, however, I find that Dr. Dawkins would surely have to know the following:

- Genesis teaches that all animals come from their own kind (operational science confirms this, but he denies this for an evolutionary presupposition). In fact, Dr. Dawkins has previously been unable to give an adequate answer as to why there is no visible evidence in operational science of DNA increasing in information, and

4. Richard Dawkins, *The God Delusion* (UK: Transworld Publishers, 2006), p. 76.

he knows it. (I recommend you watch a DVD from Answers in Genesis, *From a Frog to a Prince*.)

- Genesis teaches that a global flood destroyed the world around 4,300 years ago. (Rock layers and fossil deposits confirm this, but he denies it for an evolutionary presupposition.)

- Genesis teaches that humanity was spread out in different people groups through a confusion of language. (Isolation of gene pools in people groups confirms this, but he denies it for an evolutionary presupposition.)

- He knows that Jesus Christ has had more impact in this world than any other man in history. (He accepts it only to ridicule Christians and blame the name of Christ for wars and atrocities.)

And we could continue. It is a simple point. Dr. Dawkins and many like him actually have the truth in front of them, but they are blinded to it and see it as foolishness. Yet while he is alive there is hope for Dr. Dawkins and I am praying for his salvation. (Join me.)

At this stage it is important for me to give you some of my own testimony. I grew up in a home where my father stood solidly on the authority of the Bible. I can remember asking my father questions and having him quote Scripture to me as the answer. We would often listen to the world's philosophies and then take time to look at the Bible's answer, and I was often overwhelmed at how the Bible had an accurate and confirmable history and made much more sense of the world than human philosophy did. Especially when my brother Ken went into creation ministry, I began to see more and more that the physical evidence in the realms of biology, astronomy, geology, and anthropology matches biblical history. My father and mother were careful to help me understand the message of the gospel and the need for my response to that message. In fact, I am eternally grateful to both my parents for helping me to know the truth of God's Word and the amazing wonder of my Creator and Savior. I am thankful I learned that I could trust the Bible. In saying that, I have to admit something to all readers. My gift of faith is not of my own intellect.

Too many times in my life I have wanted to do something in complete contradiction to my understanding of the Scriptures. In fact, during a period of many years, I all but denied God's authority for my own life. My will was toward myself and not the Lord. Too many times I could dialogue with reasonable eloquence an apologetic argument to defend the Bible, and still live in total contradiction to God's expectation of conduct. It has ended in my acknowledgment that even though I understand and can reason the truth, left to my own devices, I can easily live as if it is simply foolishness. There is something in me that hits me with the desire to deny the truth of God's Word in action. If you read Romans 7, you will find it was in Paul as well. It is sin, and I cannot repel it on my own. Even though it is vitally important that we be able to declare a defense for the faith we have in Christ, it is equally vital that we understand that left to human reason alone, we will not turn to Christ and His salvation. To accept God's work of salvation through faith, we still require a higher authority. If it was just an acceptance of an exceptional amount of evidence and reason according to scriptural authority that saves us, I could claim something of myself and feel superior to fellow humans such as Dr. Dawkins. Alas, I cannot. As much as anyone in this world, a saving faith in God has not come from my own merit. I cannot claim any work or intention of my own to claim Christ as if it is me who has saved myself. I cannot conquer my own sin.

The Bible makes it totally clear: "The heart is deceitful above all things and desperately wicked" (Jer. 17:9). "And you He made alive, who were dead in transgressions and sins" (Eph. 2:1). "For the message of the cross is foolishness to those who are perishing . . ." (1 Cor. 1:18). With a wicked heart, being the walking dead and finding the message of the Cross utter foolishness, how can any man turn to God for salvation? It is impossible. The world finds

Christ and His gospel to be absolute folly and nothing more. Why should we expect differently from Dr. Dawkins and so many of his companions? Why should we expect differently from a graffiti artist teasing Alexamenos for worshiping a donkey? Why should we expect differently from the lawyer, Clarence Darrow, who wanted to abolish Christian thinking from education because he saw it as a fairy tale? And why should we expect differently of ourselves that even though the facts may be before us we struggle to live holy lives acceptable to God? Our sinful position should not bring to us surprise that we wish as a human race to deny God and seek self. That is what sin has always been by definition.

We come now to the authority of the Holy Spirit. Yes, it has been a build-up, I know. Yet it is only in acknowledging the world we live in and our position in sin that we can truly see our need for the authority of the Holy Spirit. Without His authority, we are without turning point. We are born in foolishness and self-seeking. It is only through the Holy Spirit and His authority over our lives that we can turn to God's wisdom and salvation.

Think of these points:

1. *God's Word is given to us by the Holy Spirit delivering it through His chosen men.* "Knowing this first, that no prophecy of Scripture is of any private interpretation, for prophecy never came by the will of man, but holy men of God spoke as they were moved by the Holy Spirit" (2 Pet. 1:20–21).

2. *Christ's gospel is delivered to us by the Holy Spirit bringing it to us through His mission in men (starting with the Apostles).* "But you shall receive power when the Holy Spirit has come upon you; and you shall be witnesses to Me in Jerusalem, and in all Judea and Samaria, and to the end of the earth" (Acts 1:8).

3. *We are convicted of our sin by the Holy Spirit.* "And when He has come, He will convict the world of sin, and of

righteousness, and of judgment: of sin, because they do not believe in Me; of righteousness, because I go to My Father and you see Me no more; of judgment, because the ruler of this world is judged" (John 16:8–11).

4. *The Holy Spirit opens our eyes to the truth of the gospel, and He has the authority to do so proceeding from the Father and the Son.* "I still have many things to say to you, but you cannot bear them now. However, when He, the Spirit of truth, has come, He will guide you into all truth; for He will not speak on His own authority, but whatever He hears He will speak; and He will tell you things to come. He will glorify Me, for He will take care of what is Mine and declare it to you. All things that the Father has are Mine. Therefore I said that He will take of Mine and declare it to you" (John 16:12–15). "But God has revealed them to us through His Spirit. For the Spirit searches all things, yes, the deep things of God. For what man knows the things of a man except the spirit of the man which is in him? Even so no one knows the things of God except the Spirit of God. Now we have received, not the spirit of the world, but the Spirit who is from God, that we might know the things that have been freely given to us by God" (1 Cor. 2:10–12).

5. *If the Holy Spirit does not dwell in us, we are simply not saved.* "But you are not in the flesh but in the Spirit, if indeed the Spirit of God dwells in you" (Rom. 8:9). This also shows that every true believer receives the Holy Spirit, and this is not separate from conversion.

6. *The Holy Spirit does a work of sanctification (helping us to become godly, holy, righteous).* "And such were some of you. But you were washed, but you were sanctified, but you were justified in the name of the Lord Jesus and by the Spirit of our God" (1 Cor. 6:11).

Like the Father and the Son, there are many Scriptures show-ing the deity of the Holy Spirit, and those Scriptures see the Holy Spirit as a distinct person in the Trinity. At the same time, the divine attributes of the Spirit are displayed in omnipotence, omnipresence, and omniscience.

For now, however, even though these attributes of the deity of the Holy Spirit show and prove His authority, it is important we understand this vitally important point. We completely rely on the Holy Spirit having the authority of the all-powerful God to turn us to Christ and His Word. E.H. Andrews says it this way:

> Without the Spirit to apply the atonement, we should never know its efficacy. Without the Spirit to awaken us to the fact of an offended God, we should remain heed-less, dead to all spiritual reality. Without the Spirit to stir our long-dead consciences and empower us to turn from idols and our sin, there would be no repentance (1 Thess. 1:9). Without His operation in our hearts, there would be no implanted faith, by which alone we may be saved (Eph. 2:8–9). Without His power, we could not be raised from spiritual death to new life in Christ (Rom. 8:13).[5]

All wisdom and knowledge — not just any wisdom and knowl-edge, but saving wisdom and knowledge — come through the authoritative work of the Holy Spirit in our lives. Without a submis-sion to the workings of the Holy Spirit in his life, Richard Dawkins will never cope with the evidence for the Bible's history. Without the submission to the workings of the Holy Spirit on their lives, the Supreme Court in America will never allow God's name back into the classrooms of our educators. Without the submission to God the Holy Spirit, the Church will not be sanctified and live by His truth.

It is the work of the Holy Spirit that allows us to seek God's saving wisdom. To the world it is foolishness, stupidity, ridiculous.

---

5. E.H. Andrews, *The Promise of the Spirit* (Darlington, UK: Evangelical Press, 1982), p. 17.

So be it. Here is God's answer:

> But God has chosen the foolish things of the world to put
> to shame the wise, and God has chosen the weak things of the
> world to put to shame the things which are mighty; and the
> base things of the world and the things which are despised
> God has chosen, and the things which are not, to bring to
> nothing the things that are, that no flesh should glory in His
> presence. But of Him you are in Christ Jesus, who became for
> us wisdom from God — and righteousness and sanctification
> and redemption — that, as it is written, "He who glories, let
> him glory in the LORD" (1 Cor. 1:27–31).

We have an amazing God. He is perfectly in authority over all
His creation. He not only is the just judge, but the merciful and
gracious sacrifice and the loving influence to turn us away from the
things of this world to His great salvation. While the world sees it
as folly and stupidity, God's wisdom will ring true for eternity while
those remaining unrepentant prolong under God's eternal wrath. It
is God who makes the fools wise to accept His foolishness that is
wiser than the wisdom of man (1 Cor. 1:25).

In this there is also a warning to the Church. If we are God's
people, indwelt by the Holy Spirit who has opened our eyes to His
salvation, shouldn't we then apply our honor of Him to all aspects
of truth and wisdom? Whenever we seek the wisdom of men over
the wisdom of God in any area, we are surely denying the sanctify-
ing work of the Holy Spirit in our lives. So many areas of God's
Word are foolishness to men, and many in the Church have chosen
to change God's message rather than authentically preach God's
message and respect the authority of the Holy Spirit to change the
heart of the listener.

A great example of this can be seen in a well-distributed book
called *The Lost Message of Jesus*. In this book, the author correctly
recognizes that the substitutionary atonement message of the Bible
is not easy for the world to accept. By this I mean that the world

has not easily accepted that Christ is the substitute in our place to take God's wrath that is upon us because of sin. The world does not wish to accept a wrathful God, nor that He would punish His own Son. So in order to make the world more at ease with the gospel, the author wrote a slightly different gospel, and by doing so he dismisses the authority of the Holy Spirit over the lives of the listeners. He writes:

> The fact is that the cross isn't a form of cosmic child abuse — a vengeful Father, punishing his Son for an offense he has not even committed. Understandably, both people inside and outside of the Church have found this twisted version of events morally dubious and a huge barrier to faith. Deeper than that, however, is that such a concept stands in total contradiction to the statement "God is love." If the cross is a personal act of violence perpetrated by God towards humankind but borne by His Son, then it makes a mockery of Jesus' own teaching to love your enemies and to refuse to repay evil with evil. The Truth is, the cross is a symbol of love. It is a demonstration of just how far God as Father and Jesus as His Son are prepared to go to prove that love. The cross is a vivid statement of the powerlessness of love.[6]

The Lost Message of Jesus might call substitutionary atonement a twisted event, but in doing so it teaches a powerless love and a God who would prove His love by allowing His own Son to be an impotent criminal on a Cross. This is opposite to the teaching of the Bible that tells us that not only did Christ determine to be there as His purpose for coming but that He did, in fact, do so to take the full brunt of God's wrath in our place. "In this is love, not that we loved God, but that He loved us and sent His Son to be the propitiation for our sins" (1 John 4:10).

---

6. Steve Chalke and Alan Mann, *The Lost Message of Jesus* (Grand Rapids, MI: Zondervan, 2003), p. 183.

The teaching of the Bible is that Jesus is the propitiation for our sins. This means simply that Jesus "took the full brunt of God's wrath" for our sins. Other translations use the word "atonement." But the truth is that all through the Bible God is pointing us to the substitutionary atonement of Christ. The Jewish sacrificial system pointed to Him, many accounts are a representation of Him (such as Noah's ark), the prophets foretold it, and Jesus Himself prayed about what was to come the night before it happened.

Given that *The Lost Message of Jesus* is a book that has been widely accepted, there are surely many well-meaning people who have considered how horrible it is for Jesus to have been a substitution for our punishment. And the truth is, it *is* horrible. This doesn't reflect an awful stigma on God. The stigma is on us. We are the sinners who deserve that place on the Cross. Jesus didn't impotently die to show some misdirected application of love. In full authority Jesus placed Himself on the Cross to be the sinless sacrifice that only He could be for our eternal salvation. This is love, and this is the way the gospel writers and all the Apostles' letters in the New Testament saw it. It is a horrible and terrible truth and yet with understanding given through the Holy Spirit authoritatively opening our eyes, it is a glorifying, wonderful truth.

It is a tragedy in Christian circles today that instead of accepting and teaching God's Word as our axiomatic authority, we are looking to reduce the truth of God's Word to meet the approval of more humans. Sometimes, in effect, we are reducing the truth of God's Word so much that the gospel is becoming unrecognizable. I wonder if it weren't pointed out, how many of us would pick up the fundamental errors in *The Lost Message of Jesus* about atonement. It is interesting to see the names of those who write endorsements for such books.

Some who have been shocked at a rejection of substitutionary atonement may, however, be less shocked at other areas where we have applied the same treatment of God's Word to appeal to the ears of men. Many people also believe that some aspects of Scripture may have less impact on the gospel message than others, but does that make them less authoritative? Are they written by a different God? Are they inspired by a different Holy Spirit? And what of our acceptance of the authority of the Holy Spirit to work His authentic message into the hearts of men? Do we truly accept that He can?

While writing this book, a new book hot off the press was given to me to read by a close friend. It is a book discussing the authority of Scripture to help people in their belief in God in an age of skepticism. As I read through this book I planned on hearing many of the same arguments and statements of scriptural authority that we have discussed. The book is *The Reason for God*:

> Since Christian believers occupy different positions on both the meaning of Genesis 1 and on the nature of evolution, those who are considering Christianity as a whole should not allow themselves to be distracted by this intramural debate. The skeptical enquirer does not need to accept any one of these positions in order to embrace the Christian faith. Rather, he or she should concentrate on and weigh the central claims of Christianity. Only after drawing conclusions about the person of Christ, the resurrection, and the central tenets of the Christian message should one think through the various options with regard to creation and evolution.[7]

I can heartily agree with the author on one point. The only way to salvation is through faith in Jesus Christ alone. We stand completely united in this fact. For all of this unity that we can praise God for, we must disagree with some of these statements written in *The Reason for God*.

In the book *The Lost Message of Jesus* we have an example of an author actually changing the clear message of the Bible to relate a more acceptable message to the world. In *The Reason for God*, we do have a clear and authentic gospel message (which truly differentiates it from the other) but are told to avoid the clear message of creation history, at least until someone understands the gospel. Even then,

7. Tim Keller, *The Reason for God* (New York: Penguin, 2008), p. 94.

the opening is for that person to consider both the biblical authoritative position and fallible human philosophy.

What do these positions say about the authority of the Holy Spirit? They say to me that God the Holy Spirit has limited authority. To me, as I read such statements as quoted from these books, I am left with two perceptions:

1. From *The Lost Message of Jesus* it seems that when the message of the Bible (and especially the gospel) does not meet with human approval, we can change the message so that it does. In this way we are not accepting that the Holy Spirit has authority to work His authentic message into the human heart and that His message is unacceptable.

2. From *The Reason for God* it seems even when we are not prepared to change the message of the gospel, we should avoid any other issue of biblical truth (viewed as controversial) that conflicts with human philosophy so that the listener can accept Christ first. In this way we seem to be at least questioning that the Holy Spirit has authority to convict someone upon hearing a part of His Word that human philosophy rejects, even if this issue is a stumbling block to the hearer of the gospel.

Furthermore, the statement quoted from *The Reason for God* suggests that there are "various options with regard to creation and evolution" for the converted. This would suggest that a new convert can have valid "options" for understanding Genesis that actually compromise the very gospel this person now believes. I am totally sure that it is never the author's intention to conflict with the actual gospel message, but his statement allows positions that do exactly that. *The Reason for God* is actually an apologetics book that has effectually stated that we do not need to deal with a specific question in relation to the earth's age on the basis of disagreement with long-age presuppositions. Apologetics, however, is all about giving answers, and we can certainly rely on God's Word to do exactly that.

I have witnessed a terrific example of the power of the Holy Spirit working in a man's life where neither the gospel message was changed for his comfort nor the creation message avoided for his focus. In fact, in answering his questions in relation to origins, he was able to focus more on the credibility of the gospel message.

My friend Joyce was not in a good place. Her husband, Ken, had terminal cancer and didn't know if his life expectancy was likely to be three months or even a year. Whatever the case, she had limited time left to spend with her Ken. Ken was the sort of person I would describe as a man's man, rough around the edges. But Ken did also have a sincere side, and if you could prove to Ken that you weren't some crazy religious nut he would be happy to talk with you. In fact, in my time of getting to know him, I became very fond of Ken indeed. Joyce's biggest fear, however, was that Ken was not saved and he was hurtling toward the day when it would count most. So Joyce, with great motivation to do so, persuaded Ken to come to a study that I was running. It was a six-week course called Answers for Life (available through Answers in Genesis), and it was designed to help people answer the questions they have about the Bible, Jesus, and salvation. We considered biblical relevance, the Trinity, the Bible and science, death and suffering, Jesus and one way to salvation and the Church, and the Second Coming of Christ.

I was wondering throughout the course how Ken was coping with the information, but it must have been going okay because he kept turning up with Joyce week after week, and with his sickness visibly affecting him it was a big deal for him to get there. We were nearly finished with the course and were discussing Jesus and salvation when Ken asked to revisit the section we did on creation. Something was in his mind from four sessions before that he couldn't release, and if he was going to consider the current session on Jesus, he was determined to clear up a great dilemma he was facing. So as was his style, he bluntly asked the question. It went something like this: "Steve, the breed of fish barramundi changes its sex midway through life to breed. Isn't this change a great proof for evolution?" Wow, in my mind I am wondering why for four sessions Ken was thinking about barramundi. (As an aside, if you are ever in Australia, make sure you try it.) One of our greatest treasures. The evidence before Ken was simply "change." Was the change in this fish contradictory to the Bible? Was it a proof for evolution? Ken and I together had a closer look at Genesis 1 and read together where God created all fish according to their kind.

The big question is, did the barramundi continue to be anything other than a barramundi after breeding? The answer was no. We discussed that all of the information that makes a barramundi exactly what it is, is already programmed in its DNA. Ken instantly realized how his education programming had affected him. He had been taught that any change, no matter how small, is a verification of evolution simply because it is change. However, in this instance, nothing changed. The barramundi simply did what it was programmed to do. We talked further about speciation and natural selection and how variation within the kind, even diverse variation, was still actually within the kind and in direct correlation to Genesis 1. The words I do remember Ken saying with conviction and finality on the matter were "That'll do me." Ken was now more able to concentrate on the authenticity of Jesus, having much more confidence in the authoritative credibility of God's word. Joyce then, in a marriage moment that she had never previously experienced, witnessed her husband accept Christ's free gift of salvation. I have never before seen Jesus use a barramundi to save someone, and I probably never will again. But time and time again I think of that event in my life where I thank God that He has given us the amazing blessing of being able to confirm the confirmable in His Word in such a powerful way. A way that He has used to bring people to His wonderful saving grace.

Ken became one of the most powerful witnesses for Jesus that I have ever seen, and with only three months to live, he was determined to make up for lost time. None of Ken's family could have a conversation with him without Ken insisting that they must give their life to Jesus. He soon went into the glorious presence of his creator where he remains today and forevermore. I thank God for his life.

God is Creator and King. This is the first truth of the gospel message. Without an explanation of God's kingship as Creator, the sinner has no concept of who we need to be restored to in relationship or what sin really means. While many would say that we do not need to explain creation in order to explain the gospel, I would suggest that it's not logical to understand the gospel without it. I would, however, agree that a person can in fact accept the gospel message without a thorough knowledge of creation, and many have. It is for brothers and sisters such as these, that this book is written for, with the purpose of assisting them to tighten the loose hinges and to say what has been left unsaid.

It is certainly true that there is an enormous amount of evidence confirming a literal history of Genesis 1, but it is the Holy Spirit who opens the mind of mankind to consider it. While it is the Holy Spirit who changes the hearts and minds of men in relation to the gospel message, it is never our place to usurp His authority by diminishing, changing, or avoiding any part of His authoritative Word. This is authority that we can rely on despite the acceptance of the modern secular academic thinking or any other thinking (the foolishness of men).

May I humbly and with great pleading ask that you consider allowing the Holy Spirit by His great and overwhelming authority to lead the hearts of the listener to the truth, rather than us attempting to change God's Word by appealing to their comfort. Yes, we want them to hear the gospel but not at the expense of the authority of God, for when we compromise His authority, we compromise the gospel we are preaching. This is one reason the Church has become irrelevant to the world. We have become inconsistent in our approach to Scripture, and often the best of us apply a confused message. I grant that the Holy Spirit can work a vision of the gospel of Christ in the eyes of the hearer even when we get it wrong. That is His grace mingled with His authority. Let us live according to the grace He has bestowed upon us by responding to Him in a truthful acceptance of His entire Word. The Holy Spirit does not require us to make His truth more appealing for the success of a conversion. Nor does He require us to avoid any biblical doctrine. He is God.

The world considers the message of the Bible foolish. I believe it, so the world considers me foolish. I also, however, submit to the authority of an all-powerful God. So I am happy that this world considers me a fool. I am a wise fool. The Holy Spirit has opened my eyes to the truth of His Word. While my dad and mum taught me, while my brothers and sisters encouraged me, while I used my own brain, while my Sunday school teachers presented me with lessons, and while my church preached the gospel, it was the Holy Spirit that pricked my heart and allowed me to see the truth of His Word and His gospel. It was the Holy Spirit with power and authority over my life that gave me desire for God and His salvation. It is the Holy Spirit with power and authority over my life molding me into the Potter's centerpiece on His grand table.

So if someone ever tells you that Steve Ham worships a donkey, you may respond that it is because of the authority of the Holy Spirit in his life that he is guilty of being that fool, but His Savior is no donkey. Then make sure you tell them the gospel with full biblical authority and allow the Holy Spirit to work authoritatively in their life.

I am so thankful that the authority of the Holy Spirit matters, and it matters to me a great deal. How about you?

Section Three

Authority in Christian Practice

Chapter 9

I Want It Now: Authority in Christian Living

Love [God] and do what thou wilt do.[1]
— *Augustine*

There is no shortage of Christian living teaching. In fact, many churches have pursued mission statements and have purposes based on this *life in Christ* as it applies to our earthly existence. You can find teaching in countless churches and books on how we can enrich our lives on earth, gain prosperous lives on earth, build a strong and healthy life, make a difference in life, live our best life, find empowerment in our life, excel in every sphere of life, be leaders in life, live in passion, courage, hope, love, and success, and be purpose filled. The vast array of teaching on the Christian life has become a minefield, and the popular authors of our time have gained fan bases that even rock stars would be proud of. In selecting our "life" mentors, the Christian consumer has an abundant freedom of choice and a range of advice with the widest of variation.

---

1. www. en.wikiquote.org/wiki/Augustine_of_Hippo#In_epistulam_Ioannis_ad_Parthos.

It's almost as if we can browse our Christian bookstores and select material on the basis of which author is going to help us get the most out of our life.

We can easily end up being more focused on how we can obtain better lives for ourselves in this world and how God can help us do that, rather than how we can obediently serve and worship God in preparation for our eternity with Him. In short, many Christian living books I have read have been more about what I can get and attain in this life rather than how I can live in worship of my Creator and Savior. It's the consumer mentality — "What can we get?" rather than "What can we give?" It leads us to the question, "If the Bible is the authority in matters of Christian living, which teaching is correct — giving our life to God now and forever, or getting it from Him now?"

In a very popular, modern Christian living book, *Your Best Life Now*, we are given seven steps to finding our full potential in the Christian life. In the introduction of this book, we find the seven steps for our best Christian life:

> In *Your Best Life Now*, we'll explore how to:
> • Enlarge your vision
> • Develop a healthy self-image
> • Discover the power of your thoughts and words
> • Let go of the past
> • Find strength through adversity
> • Live to give and
> • Choose to be happy
>
> In each of these areas you will find practical suggestions and simple choices that will help you to stay positive in your lifestyle and believe in a brighter future.[2]

They sound like steps that may appeal to us. But is that what the Bible teaches us should be the focus of our lives on earth? Is it

---

2. Joel Osteen, *Your Best Life Now* (London: FaithWords, 2004), p. 10.

our goal on earth to stay positive in life and be looking for our best life in this world? It is the modern prosperity doctrine. Not one that focuses just on being materially rich (or prosperous) but on being visionaries and empowered people that overcome adversity and live for good words like happiness, leadership, health, and excellence to give us a good life now. In contrast to this is the Christian life that many of our greatest Christian leaders have found to be constant struggle and suffering in this world. Charles Spurgeon suffered greatly with depression; so did Martin Luther. Many were poor, many were sick, many imprisoned, and many martyred. Surely there was more to Christianity for these people than what they might enjoy or succeed in within this world.

Are Christians truly meant to be victors in every adversity, to be able to reshape our lives through a new and powerful personal control and to be able to know lifelong happiness in this world as a choice? Are modern popular teachers really correct when they say, "God desires to promote you into new levels of prosperity, and He wants you to begin to water the seeds you have sown. God wants you to prepare to prosper!"[3] A good percentage of the Christian living books in our bookstores are telling us that we should seek to prosper, materially or otherwise, or in some cases both, and that we should be looking for the benefits of these things in Christ now.

LIVING ON THE BASIS OF BIBLICAL AUTHORITY

1. The Christian Life — Now

To one of our early Christian leaders, Augustine (the Bishop of Hippo), the Christian life was summed up in a fairly simple statement: "Love God and do as you please." This statement was later echoed by Martin Luther.

The statement is a fairly profound one. If we truly love God, our pleasure will be entirely in Him. Our desire will be to glorify Him, desire Him, love Him, serve Him, obey Him, live for Him, worship Him, pray to Him, read His Word — the list goes on. The

---

3. Joyce Meyer, *Prepare to Prosper* (New York: Warner Books, 1997), p. 26.

point of the statement is that we are to love the Lord our God with all our hearts and all our minds and all our souls. Matthew 22:37 tells us that this is the greatest commandment. It is all about God. He is the eternally existent Creator God whom we sinned against and who came to this earth to atone for those sins so that we might be saved through faith in Him (Jesus Christ). The point of our life is God. The meaning of our life is God. The purpose of our life is God. There is no other purpose or meaning outside of this. We are to desire God and His glory, and to reflect His glory as originally intended as He created us in His image. Through Christ's atonement for our sin and His righteousness given to us, we are again able to be a reflection of our Creator's glory in a limited capacity in this world but in a perfected capacity in the next.

In opening his letter to the Galatians, Paul writes that Jesus Christ "gave Himself for our sins, that He might deliver us from this present evil age" (Gal. 1:4). Through Jesus Christ we are delivered from this *present* evil age (or world). It is through faith in Christ and only in Christ that He has become the substitute for us in atonement and given us His righteousness to save us *from this present* world. Christ has delivered us now and not yet. This righteousness is what the Father sees in us, a reflection of His glory that will one day be perfected in us both spiritually and physically (more on that to come). The first thing we must realize is that when we are saved, we have a new life that is immediately and totally different from the life and life goals of this world. This world seeks empowerment, enrichment, prosperity, leadership, health, and happiness. The Christian has a new vision — Christ and Christ alone. We are converted now from this present age and we live for Christ and the age to come.

If we want to know about post-conversion Christian living, there is no better place to go than to Paul's letter to the Romans. Romans is a letter that outlines the entire Christian experience in the gospel of Christ in an intricately detailed manner. We see the impact of sin on our lives in the first three chapters and then move to the impact of the gospel in chapters 4 and 5 where Paul brings us to a point of gospel impact in our lives.

"Therefore having been justified by faith, we have peace with God through our Lord Jesus Christ" (Rom. 5:1). No longer are we at war with God, but in Jesus Christ we have one who has atoned for our sin and brought us through faith to peace with our Father. It is from this point that we now look to actually living as a Christian in chapters 6, 7, and 8.

> Knowing this, that our old man was crucified with Him, that the body of sin might be done away with, that we should no longer be slaves of sin. For he who has died has been freed from sin. Now if we died with Christ, we believe that we shall also live with Him, knowing that Christ, having been raised from the dead, dies no more. Death no longer has dominion over Him. For the death that He died, He died to sin once for all; but the life that He lives, He lives to God. Likewise you also, reckon yourselves to be dead indeed to sin, but alive to God in Christ Jesus our Lord. Therefore do not let sin reign in your mortal body, that you should obey it in its lusts. And do not present your members as instruments of unrighteousness to sin, but present yourselves to God as being alive from the dead, and your members as instruments of righteousness to God (Rom. 6:6–13).

In chapter 6, Paul makes the Christian life in Christ clear. We now belong to God. We no longer serve ourselves and our own desires, passions, or expectations because we are God's. Christian living, first and foremost, is a pursuit of God's holiness. We pursue God's holiness in worshiping Him, in focusing on Him, in obeying Him, and in loving Him above all. In the negative sense, as Paul puts it in Romans 6, we are to reject the sinful temptations and pursuits of self-glorification because we are no longer slaves to sin but free to love and serve God through Christ. We do not do so under our own power, but it is only through Christ and His gift of the Holy Spirit that sin no longer has dominion over us. This is the life on earth, in the present, which we have in Christ. In His power and only through Him it's a glorious life because it has nothing of the achievement of our own goals but a true desire to love and serve our Creator the way He originally intended.

Paul says nothing of being alive to the things of this world. In fact, he says we are dead to them. He does not ask us to be focused on the pursuit of happiness or prosperity, self-empowerment, or earthly destiny, but Christ and Christ alone. At this stage you might be thinking that I am disagreeable to someone actually having happiness in his or her life or even wealth, but this is not the case. I am simply pointing out that the pursuits of our Christian life are not to be the desire for these superficial earthly things but a desire for Christ. It is also a concern that many people, in attempting to proclaim a more acceptable gospel, prioritize the message as a hope and better life in this world rather than the repentance for sin through faith in Christ, who is our substitute and atoning sacrifice. It has become a gospel that has left out the most crucial elements of a message that now proclaims a menial hope in this world rather than an eternal hope through Jesus' work on the Cross. Luke 12:30–31 tells us to seek God first and these things will be added to you. Too many messages today are stating the opposite to this biblical truth. We should not seek things and then tack God on afterward. Our primary reason and enticement for salvation is for a restored relationship with our Creator, whom we have sinned against, that we might glorify His name.

When writing to Timothy, Paul instructs Timothy that "godliness with contentment is great gain" and further says that "we brought nothing into this world, and . . . we can carry nothing out." It further says that "those who desire to be rich fall into temptation and a snare, and into many foolish and harmful lusts which drown men in destruction and perdition" (1 Tim. 6:6–9). Paul also gives instructions to the rich to be generous. Therefore, I am not saying that happiness or wealth or health or other human enrichments in this life are not good. I am, however, saying that these are not the point of true enrichment of the Christian life nor are they the goal of such. A Christian life lived according to the authority of the Word of God is one that has all physical, emotional, and spiritual investment in God and His eternal glory. This is the only investment that can provide true riches — the richness in being content in our eternal Creator and a desire to reflect His glory. We are dead to sin, we are dead to this world, and we are alive in Christ. Jesus paid our price to allow that contentment to be our hope forever.

> I find then a law, that evil is present with me, the one who wills to do good. For I delight in the law of God according to the inward man. But I see another law in my members, warring against the law of my mind, and bringing me into captivity to the law of sin which is in my members. O wretched man that I am! Who will deliver me from this body of death? I thank God — through Jesus Christ our Lord! So then, with the mind I myself serve the law of God, but with the flesh the law of sin (Rom. 7:21–25).

If you find it amazing that Paul struggled with sin, I suggest you take great comfort in it. Paul found himself doing the things that he shouldn't do and also found himself not doing the things that he should. Sound familiar? The Christian life *now* is a life lived in a sin-corrupted world because even though we are saved from it, we still currently live in a present, evil world. We are by no means perfect in this world. We take the righteousness of the one who is. The main point of Romans 7 is to bring us into the real world of Christian living. While in chapter 6 Paul explains that we are to live as dead to sin and alive to Christ, in chapter 7 we are told that sin will always be at our door. God made the tempting power of sin clear from the beginning. In Genesis 4:6, God tells Cain that sin is at his door and has a desire for him but he should rule over it. In a sense, this is Romans 6 and 7 in one statement. No matter where we go, Romans 7 will be true for us and sin will be at our door with great desire to conquer us. In saying this, we are to live in Romans 6 as being dead to sin and alive in Christ. It is a great reminder to us that we have no authority over sin and that we need to rely on the living authority of Christ in our lives. This does not mean that we do not have responsibility — we do. We simply cannot conquer sin on our own. Only a Christian has a desire to do so because only a Christian has the authority of Christ in his life and the gift of the Holy Spirit working within us.

Our life in this world as a child of God needs to be one of self-watch, not self-esteem. We need to constantly be distrusting of our own desires and consider all in the light of Scripture and God's authority. We only need look to our globally telecast past where we have seen many of us given over to that sin of being men of great popularity and power. Sin is not discriminatory. Whether we are presidents, pastors, kings, or servants, sin is at our door. Paul is clearly telling us to live with a healthy distrust for our sinful being, and in the light of Christ's authority and the Holy Spirit in our life, to be on a serious self-watch.

> There is therefore now no condemnation to those who are in Christ Jesus, who do not walk according to the flesh, but according to the Spirit. For the law of the Spirit of life in Christ Jesus has made me free from the law of sin and death. For what the law could not do in that it was weak through the flesh, God did by sending His own Son in the likeness of sinful flesh, on account of sin: He condemned sin in the flesh (Rom. 8:1–3).

It is because of chapter 7 that chapter 8 is so wonderful. We are considered completely guilty in sin and deserving of the judgment applied to our transgressions. But in the great mercy and grace of Christ, we are not condemned. To be worthy of condemnation and yet receive mercy is the greatest enrichment of the Christian life. Paul had just finished telling us how he continues to sin and how it affects his desire to serve God, but Christ's salvation has pardoned him from the condemnation he deserves. We live in this pardoned state. It is one that should have us wanting to live for Christ out of great gratitude. Our mighty God, whom we have sinned against, has pardoned us through Christ. It is overwhelming and amazing, and it is only possible to believe on the credible authority of Scripture. When we can, and I do, it is simply the only news worth telling anyone. My God has not forsaken me because His own Son took that punishment in my place. Hallelujah! What a Savior!

I write this passage with the greatest of joy. Despite any sadness, depression, lack of wealth or status, or even without any control of our earthly destiny, we can have eternal joy (as opposed to temporal happiness). It has only been within recent history that one of my brothers has been persecuted and hurt beyond anything that I have seen in the Western Christian community, but I have still found him with this same joy. I myself have known what it means to be depressed but still experience a real eternal joy in my life. Praise God. This is the Christian life now. It may not always find us full of happiness, wealth, control, health, empowerment, or leadership, but it is certainly full of joy because of Romans 8.

I hold to these truths because I can trust the Bible implicitly. These truths are the map of life for me. I desire God. My pleasure is in Him. My Christian life now is to love God because He first loved me. It is no wonder to me that we read Paul often just gushing in praise to the Almighty as he writes his epistles. It is how I feel now because His love and His truth reach the depths of our hearts that no other could reach, and I am satisfied. I do not care how much money I have. I am not concerned about success in this world. My success is measured only in my obedience to my Lord and I will have it no other way. Any other measurement is a useless temporary tool. By the authority of God's Word there is no satisfaction in this world equal to Jesus Christ, and in fact, when we take His Word authoritatively we find that we are to desire no superficial earthly thing (even good things) above Him. I implore you to know Him. He is the Savior who is worth far more than this world.

Romans 8:31–39 finishes with the epitome of God's authority in our Christian life:

> What then shall we say to these things? If God is for us, who can be against us? He who did not spare His own Son, but delivered Him up for us all, how shall He not with Him also freely give us all things? Who shall bring a charge against God's elect? It is God who justifies. Who is he who condemns? It is Christ who died, and furthermore is also risen, who is even at the right hand of God, who also makes intercession for us. Who shall separate us from the love of Christ? Shall tribulation, or distress, or persecution, or famine, or nakedness, or peril, or sword? As it is written: "For Your sake we are killed all day long; we are accounted as sheep for the slaughter." Yet in all these things we are more than conquerors through Him who loved us. For I am persuaded that neither death nor life, nor angels nor principalities nor powers, nor things present nor things to come, nor height nor depth, nor any other created thing, shall be able to separate us from the love of God which is in Christ Jesus our Lord.

There is certainly no condemnation for those in Christ Jesus because there is no higher authority than Jesus. No accuser is above God and certainly not the great accuser, Satan. God is for us and He is the one who is the ultimate judge and He is the one who has pardoned us. There is no higher court of appeal. No matter what amazing argument one might put up, Jesus Christ is our eternal, accepted substitute. The great judge has spoken. This is what Paul also says to the Corinthians. "But with me it is a very small thing that I should be judged by you or by a human court. In fact, I do not even judge myself. For I know nothing against myself, yet I am not justified by this; but He who judges me is the Lord" (1 Cor. 4:3–4).

If we are wondering about authority and the Christian life, this crescendo in Romans that becomes the pinnacle of God's great authority as the pardoning Judge says it all. Our life is His. He not only created it, He paid for it — with His blood. There is no satisfaction in this world apart from knowing Christ. Nobody can take it from us, and the final word of pardon has already been determined through Christ. Why then desire any lower earthly richness when we are already heirs in eternity with the great I AM and sealed under His true and just authority?

2. The Christian Life — Not Yet

In this book, we have looked at God's authority and particularly at how God's authority has been evident and alive in His Word, the Bible. We have seen that His history is confirmable and sheds wonderful light on the physical evidence of this world. We have seen foretold promises fulfilled in Jesus Christ. Yet even the confirmable (which humans seem to need) is nothing in comparison to the self-authenticating claim of authority from an eternally existent Creator. God's steadfast faithfulness has been proven to us over and over in the confirmable credibility of His history, the fulfillment of His promises (especially in the Cross), and the consistent quality of His character. It is under this authentic authority that the Christian can live for Christ not only in this life but also in confidence in God's promises of the life yet to come. In this way, the Christian life is always forward-looking. Our abundant life in Christ starts in this life at the hour of our conversion and is perfected when we are taken home for eternity. In Christ we live for eternity now and yet we long to live in eternity.

We live for eternity now (in this age or world):

- Christ will be with us to the end of the age, especially in carrying out His Great Commission (Matt. 28:20).

- Christians are expected to live godly lives in this age (Titus 2:12).

- Christians should live as worthy of the coming Kingdom (1 Thess. 2:12).

- Christians are not to live as though belonging to this world (Eph. 2:2).

- Christians are not to be conformed to the pattern of this world (Rom. 12.2).

These are just a few, but we could list many Scriptures about life in this age compared to the one to come.

The point for Christians is that we live in expectation of Christ's return and His Kingdom to come. We know that His authority is also over the future. We pray "Your kingdom come, Your will be done on earth as it is in heaven," we remember it through ordinances ("for as often as we eat the bread and drink the cup we proclaim the Lord's death till He comes"), and Christians watch eagerly for Christ's return. There are so many Scriptures dealing with the return of Jesus. He foretold of His return throughout His own ministry and left us with the expectation of His coming. The gospels constantly refer to it and so do the letters of the Apostles Paul, Peter, and John.

This is how the great preacher Charles Spurgeon considered Christ's return in his own life:

His coming should be to us not only a prophecy assuredly believed among us, but a scene that is pictured in our souls and anticipated in our hearts. My imagination has often set forth that awesome scene; but better still, my faith has realized it. I have heard the chariot wheels of the Lord's approach, and I have endeavored to set my house in order for His reception. I have felt the shadow of the great cloud that will attend Him diminishing my love for worldly things. I hear even now in my spirit the sound of the last trumpet, whose tremendous blast startles my soul to serious action and brings purpose to my life. I pray to God that

I would live more completely under the influence of that grand event![4]

Charles Spurgeon had a very high view of the authority of Scripture, and as such the expectation of the coming Kingdom of Christ was evident in his passionate Christian life in this age. The impact of the authority of Scripture on our lives in respect to the future of this world should make an immeasurable difference. We do not take lightly the return of Christ because we have truly witnessed and confirmed His faithfulness. Not only do we believe in the coming of Christ but we also long for it because the promise to Christians of what follows should fill us with inexpressible joy. It is this knowledge of the future that shapes our lives now. We should be immensely passionate in evangelism. We should be living for the Lord every hour in the expectation of His coming. We should be placing God and His Word at the forefront of our lives and fearing only Him. We should be accepting what Christ told us about this present age, and we should not be fearing those who can break body or bones but only the great Judge of the universe who has total authority over eternity. This is the joyous life under the authority of God.

As previously stated, Spurgeon suffered under great depression, but his joy in the words above is evident. He did not obtain a great victory over his depression in this world. Neither did Paul obtain victory over the thorn in his side that he complained of. Whether depressed, poor, sick, a servant, persecuted, or even martyred, our victorious joy is in Jesus now and yet to be on the day of His return that we eagerly await for.

AUTHORITATIVE BOLDNESS

In 2004 a document was principally written by Dr. Patrick Sookhdeo for the Luasanne committee for World Evangelism on the Persecuted Church. Dr. Sookhdeo is an expert in this field and

---

4. Charles Spurgeon, *Grace and Power* (New Kensington, PA: Whitaker House, 2000), p. 517.

has been both active and effective in helping the persecuted church in the world.

Within the Lausanne paper an outline was given of the known persecution in the Church. It was broken down into many different sections, and following is a snippet of some of the methods of persecution reported.[5]

Islam

In some countries it is the government and its organs that persecute Christians through unjust laws, restrictions on church activities, arbitrary arrest, torture, and imprisonment. An extreme example is Saudi Arabia where all non-Muslim public religious practice is banned. In several Muslim countries, such as Saudi Arabia, Qatar, Iran, and Sudan, the law specifies the death sentence for a Muslim who converts to another religion such as Christianity. In some countries, vocal Islamists are pressuring governments to become more Islamic, implement sharia, and take a more negative stance toward Christians.

Following incitement by radical preachers and local authorities, communal and mob violence has repeatedly erupted against Christians in various countries.

Hindu

In terms of outright violence toward Christians, pastors are whipped, spat upon, and murdered. Catholic nuns are raped, and a pastor's wife was kidnapped in 2004. Evangelists are stoned and ridiculed. A group of women who had converted to Christianity in one village had their heads shaved and were forced out of the village. Church buildings have been burned in many places.

Communist Countries

Communist governments increasingly use the "rule of law" to persecute the Church, such as laws banning the

5. http://www.barnabasfund.org/pdfdocs/LOP32_IG3.pdf.

possession and distribution of information harmful to the
State. Another common method is using zoning laws to jus-
tify the closure of house churches.

It is when we look at persecution that we see the authority
of God at work in the Christian life. There are literally millions of
people on earth today that are facing poverty and imprisonment,
ridicule, exile, and even martyrdom for the sake of Christ. They
are not interested in life enrichment in this world, nor are they
concerned about taking control over their careers or friendships.
They are concerned to stay strong in the faith and not to deny their
Savior. They are claiming the joy and victory in Romans 8, and they
do not see any need to be ashamed of their position. They are like
Paul who wrote from jail:

> Therefore do not be ashamed of the testimony of our
> Lord, nor of me His prisoner, but share with me in the suf-
> ferings for the gospel according to the power of God, who
> has saved us and called us with a holy calling, not according
> to our works, but according to His own purpose and grace
> which was given to us in Christ Jesus before time began,
> but has now been revealed by the appearing of our Savior
> Jesus Christ, who has abolished death and brought life and
> immortality to light through the gospel, to which I was
> appointed a preacher, an apostle, and a teacher of the Gen-
> tiles. For this reason I also suffer these things; nevertheless I
> am not ashamed, for I know whom I have believed and am
> persuaded that He is able to keep what I have committed to
> Him until that Day (2 Tim. 1:8–12).

Paul stood strong in the face of persecution and boldly proclaimed Christ because he was convinced and reasoned and knew
whom he believed in. This is God's authority and biblical authority
working out in the Christian life. We can have boldness in our life
for Christ for there is no higher authority that calls us to serve, and

it is something that we can have complete confidence in because the authority is truly authentic and confirmable.

Our brothers and sisters in the persecuted Church have no need for Western philosophy in Christian words. They require our prayers for their support and practical support in whatever way we can provide it. But they are already victors in Christ.

Sometimes we consider our own plight in this world, and particularly in the Western world we believe will not see the same persecution against the Church. But the beginning of persecution in the Western world is well under way.

Further, in the Lausanne paper we are referred to a new Western persecution happening in our societies.

SECULARISM

A component part of the "religion" of "secularism" is sexual libertarianism and the pragmatic refusal to permit alternative structures of allegiance (such as duties toward religious organizations). In this area, our traditional freedoms premised upon Judeo-Christian thought patterns are in direct conflict with the values of the "religion" of "secularism." Unfortunately, secular society lacks its self-professed tolerance to those religious organizations that dissent from this view.

The traditional understanding of North American society is that "freedom of religion" means the freedom for religious institutions from unwarranted intrusion of the state. In Europe, this principle is inverted to mean freedom of the state from the Church.

I wonder how we will stand when one day giving account to a Western court for preaching sexual purity from our pulpits. There is a gap between the state and Christian values that was not evident in the time of our founding fathers (particularly in the USA). This gap is widening to the degree that it is becoming illegal to preach certain parts of the Bible because they might offend a community group holding to opposing values. What will happen when we are called to stand to account? Will we bow to the authorities of this world or will we be convinced in the highest authority who has called us eternally?

Already in Australia in the last decade two Christian pastors were required to fight for their freedom for teaching their congregations about Islam. They broke vilification laws in the state of Victoria. They were simply teaching their congregations what the Quran teaches and how to reach out to their fellow Muslim citizens for Christ. Both men stood firmly convinced of the authority of Scripture. They would rather answer to God. This is more of what we should expect in the Christian life. Persecution in this world is even becoming more prevalent for people who are prepared to accept that there is a designer God. A recent movie documentary by Ben Stein, the famous speechwriter and comic actor, researched scientists in the world who could not argue that the evidence points to a Creator. These scientists have been persecuted by the secular science community for doubting Darwinian evolution.

For Christians, navigating through life propelled by the power of God's Word will certainly bring persecution. We should start considering this to be normal Christian living. Not only this, but we are told to rejoice in it for the sake of Christ our Savior.

It is truly with a solid authoritative stance that we as Christians can confidently steer our way through life and sometimes willingly and knowingly through the darkest of trials. The Bible gives us reasons as to why we should believe the gospel and provides guidance for living that gospel out in our lives.

The authority of God in the Christian life can be summed up this way: our lives are completely transformed when we are saved by Christ through faith in Him. From that day forward our lives are not to be earth-centric but eternally Christ-centric. No longer do we live for material or even non-material prosperity. His authority is all that matters over every other claim of authority in this world. His eternal blessing both now and not yet is exceedingly superior to any desired blessing we may obtain on earth. We are strangers in this world with our real home yet to come. As such, we boldly

stand for His truth and we boldly live to spread this saving truth
to others in obedience to Him. We live this life with all of the per-
secutions, sicknesses, tragedies, and dissatisfaction that this world
throws at us, but we live it with a fullness of eternal joy to the glory
of our Savior. We live joyously even in our sadness and sufferings.
Our desire is not for a life that provides temporal satisfaction in
this world but only for the eternal satisfaction that is in Jesus. We
live by His authority. We live for Him. This world is not our home.
Our home, satisfaction, and life are in Christ alone. He provides the
drive, the navigation, and the destination.

Let us live our lives boldly and joyously under His authority,
His way. Let's give our lives to Him.

Chapter 10

Worship through a Torn Curtain: Authority and Worship

You shall have no other gods before Me. —
(Exod. 20:3)

Every one of us is, even from his mother's
womb, a master craftsman of idols.[1] *— John*
Calvin

In my local area over the last ten years the Muslim population has been increasing. New mosques have been built and two years ago the Australian prime minister personally opened a large private Islamic school located within three miles of where I lived. The Muslim population in that area is also strongly focused on Islamic outreach to the community. They regularly have open days at the local mosque and hold events in public parks for the local community to attend.

Even though this has happened over ten years, it seems as if the Muslim population in that local area has sprung up overnight and taken everyone by surprise. I quickly realized the need to equip

---

1. www.brainyquote.com/quotes/authors/j/john_calvin.html.

myself in the understanding of Islam and what we can do to reach out to our new neighbors. During this time we made some Muslim friends, and my wife, who is a fitness trainer, was learning how to effectively reach out to many Muslim ladies who were her clients (and friends). Three years ago one of my Muslim friends asked me to come to one of their public events. I cautiously agreed but took a Christian friend with me for support. At this event we listened to an address given by a Muslim sheik. He spoke of the great wonders of creation from the marvelous expanse of the universe to the intricacy of the smallest organisms. He was essentially asking those present to consider the amazing diversity of creation and the wonder and awe of it. He then described that the God of this creation must be amazing and we need a system to worship that God. He then described the system of the five pillars of Islam.

There is one thing that I can agree upon with the sheik. The God of this universe in all of His creative authority must be worshiped. From an understanding of creation we discover wonderful truths in respect to worship, but we do not obtain it by looking at creation alone and it cannot be explained by the five pillars of Islam or by imitating the life of the deceased human prophet Muhammad. It is only through the revelation of God's Word, the Bible, that we understand the confirmable history of creation and find true worship of that Creator.

In this chapter we will look at our need to worship God in response to His authority as Creator over all things, and as such we will start by looking at how God originally intended worship in a perfect creation. We will also understand that worship, therefore, is to be on the basis of God's design as the authority, and not our own. In this way we should be able to answer the question, "How does God's authority impact our lives of worship?"

This chapter will only skim the surface, but it is my desire for us to consider that our lives are originally and primarily purposed for the worship of the one true God who is Father, Son, and Holy Spirit. Before we begin considering how God's authority impacts our understanding and application of worship, we should attempt to define the word.

Worship in the Oxford English dictionary[2] is defined as follows:

- (noun) 1 — the feeling or expression of reverence and adoration for a deity. 2 — religious rites and ceremonies. 3 — great admiration or devotion. 4 — (His/Your Worship) chiefly Brit. a title of respect for a magistrate or mayor.
- verb (worshipped, worshipping; U.S. also worshiped, worshiping) 1 — show reverence and adoration for (a deity). 2 — feel great admiration or devotion for.

Many Christian authors have also attempted to define worship and, in fact, have written books to do just that. One of these is by David Peterson, who has written on the biblical theology of worship in an attempt to define Christian worship. Many others have done a similar thing. Peterson has hypothesized that worship is essentially *"an engagement with Him (the living and true God) on the terms that He proposes and in the way that He alone makes possible."*[3] This definition certainly encompasses an all-of-life concept of worship that would include all of the words found in the Oxford definition such as reverence, adoration, ceremony, devotion, and respect. In addition, Peterson acknowledges that true worship can only be on the terms and enabling of, and engagement with, the true and living God. True worship is not just about what we do in giving it or where we do it, but truly more important is who we give it to. David Peterson is not alone in recognizing this. Jesus also said a similar thing to the Samaritan woman in John 4:19–26:

> The woman said to Him, "Sir, I perceive that You are a prophet. Our fathers worshiped on this mountain, and you Jews say that in Jerusalem is the place where one ought to worship."

---

2. www.askoxford.com/concise_oed/worship?view=uk.
3. David Peterson, *Engaging with God* (Downers Grove, IL: InterVarsity Press) 1992), p. 20.

Jesus said to her, "Woman, believe Me, the hour is coming when you will neither on this mountain, nor in Jerusalem, worship the Father. You worship what you do not know; we know what we worship, for salvation is of the Jews. But the hour is coming, and now is, when the true worshipers will worship the Father in spirit and truth; for the Father is seeking such to worship Him. God is Spirit, and those who worship Him must worship in spirit and truth."

The woman said to Him, "I know that Messiah is coming" (who is called Christ). "When He comes, He will tell us all things."

Jesus said to her, "I who speak to you am He."

Most orthodox Christians would at least agree that true worship is given to God through salvation in Jesus Christ and encompasses a life of adoration and reverence. This is how we were originally created as worshipers. Our whole life was originally intended to be perfect worship reflecting God's image.

CREATED AS WORSHIPERS

There are many who would teach that God has created us because He needed us to worship Him. If this is the sole reason for our creation then we point to some type of lacking in God, that He needed to be worshiped. The biblical teaching about God clearly shows us that God lacks for nothing. He is eternally self-existent, sustained, and contained. The best understanding of why God has created us is to understand the immense and unlimited nature of His own glory. God created us in His own glory, and, in fact, in this we would see that creation itself is an act of God's own worship.

For any of us to consider that we could worship ourselves would be cause to accuse us of being conceited. But God is not a limited human that worship would place Him in unequal highness over others. God is God. He is the I AM. It is God who calls us to worship Him:

> Oh, the depth of the riches both of the wisdom and knowledge of God! How unsearchable are His judgments and His ways past finding out!
> "For who has known the mind of the Lord?
> Or who has become His counselor?"
> "Or who has first given to Him
> And it shall be repaid to him?"
> For of Him and through Him and to Him are all things, to whom be glory forever. Amen.
> I beseech you therefore, brethren, by the mercies of God, that you present your bodies a living sacrifice, holy, acceptable to God, which is your reasonable service (Rom. 11:33–12:1).

The Apostle Paul is explaining here that God has no need and is in fact the initiator of all life. God is the authority and He does not owe us anything. Everything, including worship, comes from Him, and it is in His mercy that we can present worship to Him through the sacrifice of our life (because of the sacrifice of Christ's life).

Before the world was created, God was. The Bible clearly teaches that the Father, the Son, and the Holy Spirit are one God and that this amazing God has been eternally present. Genesis 1:1 begins with the words, "In the beginning God. . . ." While the essence of the Trinity is far beyond our human comprehension, we can at least understand that God, within the relationship of the Trinity, did not create either out of a need for companionship or worship. Within the communion of the Trinity there is perfect love, praise, adoration, and joy. It has always been there and always will be. We see this visibly through Jesus as He lived to honor and glorify the Father. God is continually the self-fulfilled God in all respects. He is the supreme one and there is no higher authority. Mankind is a result of the overflow of His amazing worship because we were created in His image to reflect His glory.

Then God said, "Let Us make man in Our image, according to Our likeness; let them have dominion over the fish of the sea, over the birds of the air, and over the cattle, over all the earth and over every creeping thing that creeps on the earth." So God created man in His own image; in the image of God He created him; male and female He created them. Then God blessed them, and God said to them, "Be fruitful and multiply; fill the earth and subdue it; have dominion over the fish of the sea, over the birds of the air, and over every living thing that moves on the earth." And God said, "See, I have given you every herb that yields seed which is on the face of all the earth, and every tree whose fruit yields seed; to you it shall be for food. Also, to every beast of the earth, to every bird of the air, and to everything that creeps on the earth, in which there is life, I have given every green herb for food"; and it was so. Then God saw everything that He had made, and indeed it was very good. So the evening and the morning were the sixth day (Gen. 1:26–31).

By the end of the sixth day of creation, it was already evident that mankind was created in an environment of worship. We were first created in God's image and created for wonderful relationship to reflect His image as He created us male and female. We were made to perpetually reflect God's image as we were commanded to be fruitful and multiply. We were made to reflect God's image as we were given dominion over His creation. God looked at His creation and saw that it was very good. This is a wonderful picture of worship. This was the perfect glorification of God the Creator without blemish or spot. This is the worship that God rested in on the seventh day. This is the worshipful rest that the Jewish Sabbath was to represent as it reflected creation week, that became the reason we have six work days and a day of rest (Exod. 20:8–11). We live to reflect His glory in perfect worship and we are reminded of it on a weekly basis.

We see the desired nature of worship further explained as we look closer at creation:

Then the LORD God took the man and put him in the garden of Eden to tend and keep it. And the LORD God commanded the man, saying, "Of every tree of the garden you may freely eat; but of the tree of the knowledge of good and evil you shall not eat, for in the day that you eat of it you shall surely die."

And the LORD God said, "It is not good that man should be alone; I will make him a helper comparable to him." Out of the ground the LORD God formed every beast of the field and every bird of the air, and brought them to Adam to see what he would call them. And whatever Adam called each living creature, that was its name. So Adam gave names to all cattle, to the birds of the air, and to every beast of the field. But for Adam there was not found a helper comparable to him.

And the LORD God caused a deep sleep to fall on Adam, and he slept; and He took one of his ribs, and closed up the flesh in its place. Then the rib which the LORD God had taken from man He made into a woman, and He brought her to the man.

And Adam said:

"This is now bone of my bones
And flesh of my flesh;
She shall be called Woman,
Because she was taken out of Man."

Therefore a man shall leave his father and mother and be joined to his wife, and they shall become one flesh.

And they were both naked, the man and his wife, and were not ashamed (Gen. 2:15–25).

The man was to subdue the creation, till it, and use it for food, as well as the good of mankind. In consistency with being created in the image of God, man was never meant to worship the creation or hold the creation in higher esteem than God. In fact, here we see that God has given man authority over the creation. We have guardianship and responsibility, but the Lord gave it to us for our benefit in our worship of Him. Today, as we look around the world, we see so many humans worshiping the creation rather than the Creator. Mankind has worshiped almost everything in creation from the sun, to cows, to images we have made out of materials, to the environment itself. This is why John Calvin correctly stated, "Every one of us is, even from his mother's womb, a master craftsman of idols."[4]

God created us as worshipers in that even our relationships are lived in adoration of Him. He created us to be one man for one woman in perfect communion in relationship and in perfect equality in roles of leadership and submission, reflecting and honoring the trinitarian relationship of God's own essence. It is in reading the first two chapters of Genesis that we receive the greatest picture of worship (sinless worship). We were created as worshipers to reflect God's glorious image and to honor and adore Him in every action of leadership, submission, guarding, tilling, naming, procreating, and even eating.

God gave us one more way of worshiping Him . . . obedience. The differentiating factor is always that God is God the Creator and we are His creation. Our act of worship toward God was to remain and live in obedience to Him by obeying His command in the garden. We failed. The difference between living a life of true worship and living a life of false worship is about who we worship. Mankind chose self-worship by disobeying God; and ever since, we have had a worship problem. Every time we choose our own will over God's, we worship self. Every time we place something above God in importance, we worship the creation rather than the Creator. When we sinned in the garden we placed ourselves in an impossible position to worship God. We had chosen ourselves above Him, and

4. www.calvin500.com/john-calvin/quotes-by-calvin.

only in His mercy and grace in enabling us could we ever again find ability to worship God in spirit and truth.

This is our great necessity for Jesus. It is impossible for us to worship a perfect and holy God in truth from a position of sin and imperfection. The honor left to God is all of Him. He is a holy God honored in judging the rebellion of sin, and He is a gracious and merciful God honored in providing a perfect substitute, atoning for our sin, and being righteousness in our place. Through Christ alone do we have opportunity for true worship. No amount of ceremonial pomp or of heartfelt music and singing, and certainly not the five pillars of Islam, will put us in a right stead to worship our Creator. Worship for the Christian is a life lived according to the substitutionary sacrifice of Jesus. It is through worship that we again desire something that may resemble a pre-Fall relationship with God in adoration, honor, and obedience. Worship is the prime illustration of our acceptance of God's authority and our reliance on Him in our sinful condition.

Man was created perfect, able to worship God in spirit and in truth. We became imperfect, no longer able to worship God in spirit and in truth. While still living in this world we remain imperfect, but through Christ alone we can again worship God in spirit and in truth. One day we will be restored for all eternity when we will securely worship forever in spirit and in truth.

Since mankind's ejection from the Garden of Eden, even in our sinful state, God has mercifully given us the ability to worship Him. God made with us covenants of worship where He would faithfully abide with us as we live according to the one who would come as the eternal sacrifice. The first blood sacrifice is implied in the skin coverings of Adam and Eve in their shame. Abel's sacrifice was acceptable to God as a blood sacrifice whereas Cain's was not. God faithfully kept His promise to Eve in providing Jesus as the ultimate sacrificial seed. Abraham was promised to be the father of many nations and through his family would come the greatest blessing: Jesus. Moses was given the Law, and through the hardships of the desert, the Israelites made it to the Promised Land.

All of the covenant promises and faithfulness of God are evidence that God was present with His worshipers as accounted in the Old Testament. God established many things for His people to acknowledge a life of worship. If you were an Israelite you would have been reminded of living for God through the tabernacle, sacrifices, festivals, Ten Commandments, and all of the surrounding law, the constant reminder of God continuing and renewing His covenant through the coming of the Messiah. All of these things point to the fact that God has authoritatively established for us that worship is a constant living in the presence of a mighty Creator. God's presence was well established with the Israelites of the Old Testament. While only the priests could approach the Holy of Holies behind the curtain in the temple, the temple was always in the midst of God's people, and His covenant, law, sacrifices, and festivals continually surrounded it. God is within and in the midst of His people, mercifully enabling and graciously reminding of the need for worship. This is worship that has only ever been acceptable in the fulfillment of the promised sacrifice of the Lord Jesus.

GOD'S DESIGN FOR WORSHIP

The concept of worship has been one of the most hotly debated topics in the modern church. Much of the time it comes down to the style of music in the church service, which is a great pity considering we have seen that worship is so much more than the time we spend together corporately on a Sunday morning. But we have ourselves to blame. We have inappropriately named our Christian gatherings, praise singing, and even the people leading them. We go to a worship service to sing songs to God during the worship time and are led by a worship leader and the worship team (musicians). We often have people in charge of putting together the program for our meeting and call them the worship director. We even have worship pastors. Of all the terms in our modern church, I have found these terms to be the most unhelpful in allowing us to fully comprehend the concept of worship according to the authority of God. It is no surprise to me that most people see the main reason and purpose for the church gathering as worship.

Before I proceed with this subject, I must make something very clear. There is something special in worship when God's congregated family comes together. It is part of our meeting together that gives us a small glimpse of heaven when we will be gathered in continual corporate worship of our God for all eternity. In Hebrews 12:22–24 we get a description of this:

> But you have come to Mount Zion and to the city of the living God, the heavenly Jerusalem, to an innumerable company of angels, to the general assembly and church of the firstborn who are registered in heaven, to God the Judge of all, to the spirits of just men made perfect, to Jesus the Mediator of the new covenant, and to the blood of sprinkling that speaks better things than that of Abel.

We meet in the name of Christ who, unlike the first ever "lamb" sacrifice, is our one-for-all sacrifice. We meet in eternal forgiveness and we come together as God's people in a picture of what is yet to come. So it is true that there is something special in worship when God's people meet together, but we do not gather together for the purpose of worship; we already have that purpose by breathing. We come together *in* worship, not *to* worship. I am not demeaning worship in the church gathering by saying this, and at the same time I do not wish to restrict worship to the songs we sing before the Bible message.

This truly is an important consideration because the vast misunderstanding in relation to biblical worship has reduced both our capacity in worship of God and the effectiveness of our gathering together. If we are looking to the church gathering to be our requirement for worship, we have missed God's expectations by a long way. We need to understand God's expectation of both the church gathering and of worship and accept only the authority of His Word to give us this instruction.

In 1 Corinthians 11:18, Paul starts to instruct the church on its gathering together. The Corinthians were meeting with disrespect, division, selfishness, pride, and disorder. The Corinthian church had some major problems, and it was Paul's desire to instruct them on the proper purpose and structure of their church meetings. He commences with this instruction: *"For first of all, when you come together as a church. . . ."* This statement is repeated a few times throughout the next three chapters as Paul discusses the vital issues concerning the church meeting. While Paul is dealing with these problems, he not only discusses the solutions to the issues but also gives them the reason it is important to solve them. It is for the purpose of their meeting together.

Paul commences his instruction on the church gathering by calling into order those who impatiently and selfishly eat and drink the Lord's Supper for themselves, causing factions and disunity. He plainly gives instruction on this, showing that the gathering is to be united in the centrality of Jesus and His work on the Cross. Apart from this, Paul continues to teach the following about Christians gathering together at Corinth.

They were instructed to/for the purpose of the following:

Ministering to each other in the Spirit — *for the profit of all* (12:7)

Sharing their gifts and strengths with each other in a united group — *that the members should have the same care for one another* (12:25)

Having order in the church so that he who prophesies — *edifies the church* (14:4)

Having interpretation with tongues so that — *the church may receive edification* (14:5)

Using the spiritual gifts you are zealous for — *for the edification of the church* (14:12)

Praying and giving thanks so others can understand, otherwise — *the other is not edified (14:17); let all things be done for edification* (14:26)

Prophesying one by one — *that all may learn and be encouraged* (14:31)

Let all things be done decently and in order.

Anyone scrutinizing the purpose statements behind Paul's instruction would see that Paul is saying that we come together and do all things as a gathered body for the edification, care, and encouragement of all. Much of this is centered around the Word of God. Therefore, we should probably call our "worship teams" edification teams. But that, too, would limit the word "edification" to music. I hope you get the point. Our worship as a congregation is in our ability to meet together in the unity of Christ for the edification and encouragement of the body to worship Christ more fully whether together or apart. It is in this teaching that I encourage any reader to consider their gifts of grace that they bring to their local gathering. Imagine a church where we all met in worship but also with a primary purpose to encourage and edify each other in our lives of worship. Our church gathering is certainly an act of worship when we do this. Our songs that we sing are sung together in unity in Christ. In solidarity we praise God as if we will be doing it for all eternity, and we will. We seek the Lord together around the Bible to be instructed and challenged by God's authoritative Word. We serve each other in God's grace and with His individually gifted talents to seek to encourage each other to be better worshipers.

We no longer seek a temple for worship. Jesus Christ has taken this place in the most amazing way. When Jesus died on the Cross, He became the once and for all perfectly atoning sacrifice for our sin. Where at one time the Jews could only rely on the priests to be their symbolic representatives in entering into the presence of God, Jesus was given to this world as Immanuel, "God with us." He took our place on the Cross and abolished our need for any other representative forever. "And Jesus cried out again with a loud voice, and yielded up His spirit. Then, behold, the veil of the temple was torn in two from top to bottom; and the earth quaked, and the rocks were split" (Matt. 27:50–51). This is why we now worship through a torn curtain. Jesus *is* our access to worship God, not the temple, not the gathering. We no longer go "to" the house of God, we "are" the house of God.

The Jews had the Commandments, the Law, the sacrifices, festivals, and of course the central presence of the temple. Jesus fulfilled it all.

It is a great pity that many of us see the need to go back to something that Christ has fulfilled. We sometimes live as if the curtain had never been torn. We have free access to the Father through the Son, Jesus Christ (1 Pet. 2:9). He is present and has given the Holy Spirit to abide in the life of every believer. We no longer require a priest but have become a royal priesthood through Christ. With Christ's fulfilment of the law and sacrifice, we live in His grace. With this comes an enormous responsibility because we live 24/7 in the presence of our Lord and Savior, through whom we can again worship God in spirit and truth.

God in His great authority, from the moment of our Fall in the Garden of Eden, has purposed to put right our worship of Him. This is why it is so important for every Christian to see that Christ is the central theme of all Scripture. Christ is God and Creator of all and perfectly worshiped in a pre-Fall world. In the post-Fall world, Christ is the Messiah whom the festivals, sacrifices, and laws pointed to, and Christ is Immanuel, God with us. And all believers eagerly wait together for the day that He will again be worshiped perfectly for all eternity.

Worship is one of the most important concepts for a Christian to understand, and our guidance for understanding worship must be authentic. Too often a limited concept of worship is directed by a desire to make church gatherings more stylistically relevant to the community around us or by a desire to make our "worship time" an experience of holy wonder. When the practical definition of worship is confined to the style of the church service (particularly regarding music), we lose the biblical model for whole of life worship. When the practical definition of worship is influenced through a misappli-cation of terms such as "the house of God," we can too easily apply sanctity toward buildings and aesthetics rather than toward God, His Word, and our relationship with Him. When we take God's Word as the authority for worship, only then do we understand that treating church buildings and church services like the Old Testa-ment temple is actually denying the work of Christ on the Cross and the curtain torn in two. The biblical model for worship has us understanding that our regular gatherings are an important and cor-porate part of our worship where we meet in fellowship around the authoritative Word of God for the edification of the saints. We share gifts, sing hymns and spiritual songs, break bread to remember our Lord, and do all around the central element of the preaching of God's truth. We then continue our worship as individuals, families, friends, and colleagues as we live lives that seek to glorify God in all we do, understanding that our worship is only possible through the all-conquering majesty of Jesus Christ.

THE AUTHORITY OF GOD FOR INSPIRATION OF WORSHIP

If you have read through this book you will find that I am convinced of God's authority. His own claims of authority ring true in the confirmation of the confirmable. His Word has a richness and deepness like no other book, giving us a real sense of the I AM reaching out to humanity. His general revelation in creation, natu-ral law, and in a moral and religious sense shows us a world crying out His name. His special revelation in the Lord Jesus Christ and His Word, the Bible, brings us to an intimate understanding of His authentic history, creative power, redemptive desire, just wrath, and abounding grace. God has promised and faithfully delivered to His own glory, with still more to come upon His return when every knee will bow and every person will proclaim His authority as God. Sadly, some will do this in shuddering dismay for their unbelief.

How do you respond to such a God who owns everything and is in complete authority over everything because He created everything? I am hoping some of this discussion has given you some idea of a life of worship worth living. In another sense, sometimes it is just good to consider His God-ness, to put off all misconceptions of our own authority in life and give everything over to the worthiness of His praise and adoration. We must deny our own sense of pride and ambition. We must cease our misgivings of self-worth to find all pride and worth in Him our God — and then live that way.

So let's end by acknowledging that the misdirected "worship" debate over styles of music is really more irrelevant than many realize in the big picture of true worship. Let's hear wonderful words written out of worshipful hearts from both a hymn writer and a contemporary group.

Immortal, Invisible, God Only Wise

Immortal, invisible, God only wise,
In light inaccessible hid from our eyes,
Most blessèd, most glorious, the Ancient of Days,
Almighty, victorious, Thy great Name we praise.

Unresting, unhasting, and silent as light,
Nor wanting, nor wasting, Thou rulest in might;
Thy justice, like mountains, high soaring above
Thy clouds, which are fountains of goodness and love.

To all, life Thou givest, to both great and small;
In all life Thou livest, the true life of all;
We blossom and flourish as leaves on the tree,
And wither and perish — but naught changeth Thee.

Great Father of glory, pure Father of light,
Thine angels adore Thee, all veiling their sight;
But of all Thy rich graces this grace, Lord, impart
Take the veil from our faces, the vile from our heart.

All laud we would render; O help us to see
'Tis only the splendor of light hideth Thee,

And so let Thy glory, Almighty, impart,
Through Christ in His story, Thy Christ to the heart.[5]

King of Glory

Who is this King of Glory that pursues me with His love
And haunts me with each hearing of His softly spoken words,
My conscience, a reminder of forgiveness that I need,
Who is this King of Glory who offers it to me.

Who is this King of angels, O blessed Prince of Peace,
Revealing things of Heaven and all its mysteries.
My spirits ever longing for His grace in which to stand,
Who's this King of glory, Son of God and son of man.

His name is Jesus, precious Jesus,
The Lord Almighty, the King of my heart,
The King of glory.

Who is this King of Glory with strength and majesty,
And wisdom beyond measure, the gracious King of kings,
The Lord of Earth and Heaven, the Creator of all things.
Who is this King of Glory, He's everything to me.
The Lord of Earth and Heaven, the Creator of all things,
He is the King of glory, He's everything to me.[6]

Oh, the wonderful, awesome authority of our God. I am compelled to worship Him and not just on Sunday mornings.

---

5. "Immortal, Invisible, God Only Wise," Walter C. Smith, words; John Roberts, music.
6. "King of Glory," by D. Carr, M. Powell, M. Lee, T. Anderson, and B. Avery.

Chapter 11

Taking Back the Family: Authority and the Christian Family

Unless the LORD builds the house, they labor in vain who build it. — (Ps. 127:1)

The breakdown of the nuclear family has been steering our postmodern society toward moral bankruptcy. I know this is a truly disturbing comment to commence this chapter with, but if the Christian family is to claim God's authority, we need to know what we are up against. Even in my lifetime in Australia, I have noticed an amazing shift in our culture in the secularization of moral values and an acceptance of self-authority. This is the postmodern thinking, and despite having moved on from the postmodern generational era, postmodernism has reshaped Western values and especially views on religion.

In Australia, our last census was held in 2006. The statistics in relation to religion are disturbing but not really surprising. In our 1981 census, 88 percent of Australians held some form of religious belief. In 2006 religious belief has reduced to 79 percent, and a truly disturbing aspect of these census statistics relates to children from birth to age five where parents would have assigned a religion at birth. The 2006 census confirms that this assignment of family religion was done for only 63 percent of infants. It is because of this that one of Australia's most famous demographers and social commentators, Bernard Salt, makes this statement: "Godlessness, it would seem, is on the up and up and gathering momentum."[1]

Salt goes on to explain some of the characteristics of the generations that have contributed to this situation. It seems that the last generation of dual "working parents of indulgence" has given the next generation little to think about in relation to God. Our society has all but shut God out of our homes and replaced Him with the worship of lifestyle.

In our Western society our children are more and more disengaged with the church and families, and educational facilities don't seem to be leaving children with a strong enough foundation. Salt continues to state: "For the past 25 years, belief has peaked at the age of 15 while teenagers are still at school and under the influence of their parents. Thereafter, young Australians are increasingly likely to claim 'no religion' at the census."[2]

Even in our Christian families, many young people are leaving home at the same time that they leave the Church. "Disengagement" is the word that describes how children are being brought up in respect to God. They are disengaged because they see no sense in tradition. They see hypocritical behavior in Christians. They are educated in schools (even so-called Christian schools) that educate on the basis of evolutionary philosophy. They have little or no understanding of the credibility of the Bible. Little in Christianity makes sense to them, so why spend the time and energy in church. This is a major problem because when our children are disengaged

---

1. Bernard Salt, *The Man Drought* (Australia: Hardie Grant Books, 2008), p. 236–237.
2. Ibid.

with God, they are disengaged with all of the moral and faith issues that we as parents find so important. Why bother getting married? Why not live my own lifestyle? Why not do the things that make me happy and give me self-gratification?

I found it very interesting that a secular demographer such as Bernard Salt has ended up making the following statement about how he sees the future of the family unit in Australia on the basis of our census statistics: "We have seen ourselves, and still see ourselves, primarily as a nation of families. But it will not be long before the traditional nuclear family, otherwise known as mum, dad, and the kids, will cease to be the dominant social institution."[3] Australian homes are fast being filled with divorced, one-parent families, homosexual couples, de facto relationships, and shared accommodations. Statistically, the family unit is dying. It is time for the Christian family to get real and to be concerned, very concerned. We are fighting for an institution that was originally created to reflect the very glory of our Creator. The family (and particularly the Christian family) is the backbone of society. What happens when this backbone becomes irrelevant to society? Well, society becomes morally crippled.

These Australian statistics and commentary from one of our leading demographers paint a very dim picture indeed for those concerned about Australian Christian families. While some would call Australia a "Christian" nation, I do not see my country in this way. Many Aussies are prepared to be assigned a religious designation, but few of us attend church on a regular basis, and those with a life-changing acceptance of Jesus as our only true Savior would be even fewer.

When I visited the United States for the first time, I remember being surprised by the difference in culture compared to Australia. There was still some evidence that the United States has come from a "Christianized" heritage going back to some solid Christian forefathers. Even with this as what was once the foundation of a nation, a cultural change has taken place in America whereby now even the

3. Ibid.

evangelical church is losing its youth. In a George Barna survey of Christianity in the United States he states:

> Many twentysomethings are reversing course after having been active church attenders during their teenage years. As teenagers, more than half attended church each week and more than 4 out of 5 (81%) had ever gone to a Christian church. That means that from high school graduation to age 25 there is a 42% drop in weekly church attendance and a 58% decline from age 18 to age 29. That represents about 8,000,000 twentysomethings alive today who were active church-goers as teenagers but who will no longer be active in a church by their 30th birthday.[4]

My brother Ken was concerned about the cultural change in the United States and decided to get some updated data from a reputable research group to measure what is really happening in American Christian society:

> In August 2006, Answers in Genesis–USA commissioned Britt Beemer from America's Research Group[1] to find out why young people were leaving the church. Respondents indicated that Sunday school materials were shallow and "irrelevant." Of those polled, 86% had begun to question the Bible by their high school years. Of those who said they did not believe all the accounts in the Bible are true, 82% cited doubts about the Bible's authority or its trustworthiness.[5]

To see the devastating demise of Christian culture in the United States one only has to look into the prestigious universities such as Harvard, Princeton, and Yale. They were originally founded as Christian establishments but are now closed to biblical thinking.

---

4. Mark Driscoll, *Confessions of a Reformission* (Grand Rapids, MI: Zondervan, 2006), p. 10.
5. www.answersingenesis.org/articles/am/v2/n3/walking-away-from-truth.

The fact is that our children are being brought up with loose hinges on their doors of faith. (See chapter 1.) They have no answers and no authority to cling to. Schools, universities, and, sadly, even Sunday schools are not doing their jobs. Even parents are not helping their children fix their doors to a firm and solid frame of biblical authority, as they are responsible for doing. It is time that an authentic authority be brought back to the Christian family unit, and it starts with us being the husbands and wives and dads and moms that God created us to be. With God's authoritative foundations, it is time to take back the family and truly bring up a godly generation.

Taking Back Fatherhood

Sadly, there are many people in the world that cannot share the same testimony as I have about my father, but it is a great blessing that we can learn all we need about fatherhood from Scripture. In saying this, my hero of earthly fatherhood has definitely been my own father. Ken and I have spoken and written much about him. I am unashamed to pronounce him as a great Christian leader and mentor in my life.

My dad was by no means perfect, and I could certainly comment on a few areas where I believe he fell short of the mark. Then again, my children will probably say similar of me in years to come. But when the fundamentals are considered, I found very little fault in him. I believe the main reason for this is because my dad was a man of God's Word. I have many times described his view of the Bible this way: "He read it, he believed it, he defended it, he taught it, and he lived it, and he did all of this in front of his wife and children and *with* his wife and children." He was a real man. He took responsibility to earn a living for our household. He loved us in very practical ways (not always terribly affectionate, though). He defended the Word of God against liberalism, and we would often hear him use the words "thus said the Lord." He stood on biblical authority and taught us all how to do it. He was the greatest educator I had in my life. Yet if he taught me one thing, it was to not simply follow after the ways of men (even him) but to stand firm in the Word of God.

There are many verses in the Bible about fathers, and as you read through all the references you quickly find that fathers were mentioned in a multigenerational capacity. Many references are made in respect to the land of our fathers, the promise to our fathers, the sins of our fathers, and the teaching of our fathers. These things seem to be remembered for generations. Psalm 22:4 gives us a classic example of this: "Our fathers trusted in You; they trusted, and You delivered them." The biblical understanding of fathers is that so much of what we do is handed on to the next generation and the generation after that. This doesn't mean that it is us that can save our children; we all have individual responsibility before God. I can only pray that the biblical stance of my father is something that I can hand on to my children and then through to my children's children, that they may know Christ. This is the teaching we see in Psalm 78:1–7.

> Give ear, O my people, to my law; incline your ears to the words of my mouth. I will open my mouth in a parable; I will utter dark sayings of old, which we have heard and known, and our fathers have told us. We will not hide them from their children, telling to the generation to come the praises of the Lord, and His strength and His wonderful works that He has done. For He established a testimony in Jacob, and appointed a law in Israel, which He commanded our fathers, that they should make them known to their children; that the generation to come might know them, the children who would be born, that they may arise and declare them to their children, that they may set their hope in God, and not forget the works of God, but keep His commandments.

It is truly a father's job to tell the truth and counsel of God's Word to his children that it may be rightly established and his children might tell it to the next generation. This is God's will for the family, that it may be strongly rooted in His Word to deliver it to the next generation. God's greatest equipping of evangelism is here before us. Fatherhood is the great leadership and missionary role. It is education, nurturing, admonition, love, evangelism, and empowerment, and there is no way to accomplish these unless a man can lead from the front. Fathers have a truly valuable calling in introducing Jesus to their families and teaching their families to properly build strong, long-lasting hinges. It is therefore time for fathers to train themselves in order to train their families.

It is also at this point that I must mention wives. While we are discussing what fathers must do for their children, it is equally important that they lead their wives in God's Word as well. While this chapter is not going to be a full discussion on the roles of husbands and wives, it is important to note that Scripture is clear. Husbands are to love and lead their wives as Christ loves the Church, and wives are to submit to their husbands. Christ leads and loves His church. He teaches us, nurtures us, and cares for us. Christ is incredibly gracious toward us and merciful to us even when we cross Him. His love for us is perfect, and this is how the love of a husband must be for his wife. This love must surely flow in a husband's loving, teaching, and caring for his wife. It is here that we men need to ask ourselves if our children are witnessing us truly loving and caring for our wives and leading them in Scripture.

We will talk about mothers having a wonderful and respected role soon. For now, we must say that it is essential that a husband be seen as the key leader by his wife to allow her to fulfill her role in motherhood. The roles of fathers, mothers, and even children were created to display a wonderful reflection of God's glory, particularly in respect to His triune nature. God is one God and yet three persons. The Scripture often shows the Spirit in submission and yet equal to the Father and the Son, and the Son often shown in submission and yet equal to the Father. We see in Scripture that there are distinct roles and submission in the Trinity, but we also know there is total equality in that God is God. The family unit is like this. All are to be equally valued within their roles, with children submitting to parents and wives submitting to husbands. (Submission in Scripture never equates to lesser value.) It is essential, therefore, that fathers lead their families and that mothers support their husbands in willing submission so that they can be a united force in loving and caring for children who are to submit to both fathers and mothers.

While my wife and I sometimes disagree, like any married couple, I am so thankful that Trish has even in times of disagreement submitted to my leadership in the home. She would also be the first to tell you that sometimes she struggles with this, a struggle that Scripture identifies that any wife will have. I have also had to apologize to Trish many times when my decisions and style of leadership have not been on the mark. Nevertheless, I have at least by experience learned to listen to her more. Yet she has continued to respect God's role for me as the spiritual leader for the sake of obeying God and providing a united front for teaching and caring for our children. This has worked out for us in some very practical ways. Just recently we were together in a local Christian bookstore. While I was having fun in the apologetics section, Trish came to me with a few suggestions for a devotional book for her. She was concerned to make sure the author and book she was selecting was going to be in line with the biblical doctrine taught in our home. In front of our daughter, I was able to give some good reasons for my suggestion and was able to passively teach some discernment. I know that Trish is discerning enough to know when she is hearing something not in line with scriptural truth, but I was totally encouraged that she respected me as the spiritual leader in our home by asking for my opinion and doing it in front of our daughter.

Unfortunately, in many homes the spiritual headship has been given over by husbands to wives. This is not the biblical model at all. It is time to take back fatherhood. Not a forceful, exasperating fatherhood (as warned against in Ephesians 6:4) but a fatherhood that cares enough for wife and children that he would nurture, love, care for, and teach within the truth of God's Word.

TAKING BACK MOTHERHOOD

Unfortunately, our world has valued motherhood as a menial position in life. We have *underestimated* the value of mothers. Instead of reducing the material lifestyle assets that consume our incomes, many have demanded that women place their role of motherhood as a secondary position to income earner for the provision of things or maintenance of debt. This is why Bernard Salt described modern parents as "working parents of indulgence."[6] Parenting (for both fathers and mothers) has become second place to *provisioning* and, sadly, *ego*. This is not stated to rebuke working mothers — not in the least. It's about attitude. Does the care and nurture of our children come first, or things? For many, a double income is necessary just to pay the bills and keep food on the table. For others, well, it must be a choice of Scripture-enlightened conscience.

In saying this it must also be stated that Scripture does not prohibit mothers from working. Proverbs 31 states very clearly that while living in the safe trust of her husband, a mother loses no capacity for industrious commerciality. Many moms choose to work, considering it God's calling as part of their primary purpose as a resourceful mother (again, this must be a matter of Scripture-enlightened conscience). In many households today, moms are required to work, and some even full-time for the sake of their family's needs. Many of these moms are even single parents. Being a single parent is immensely difficult. We live in a sin-cursed world where many sadly find themselves in broken family circumstances, through either death, divorce, or past or even present sin. It is these circumstances where the care and counsel of the Church is essential. Whether a matter of choice or need, the point we need to clearly delineate is the "value" we place on motherhood. While Proverbs

---

6. Salt, *The Man Drought*.

31 shows an industrious mother, it also shows a mother who has immense care for the provision, care, and nurture of her family. These are not the ambitions of the feminist movement, they are the ambitions of a godly woman who applies the authority of Scripture to her life.

Taking back motherhood under the authority of God means first seeing motherhood the way God has shown us in His Word. It means to first accept that motherhood is not just an adequate role or a menial duty but a treasured, crucial, and essential high calling. Reading through Proverbs 31, we soon realize that this description of a godly wife and mother is of a truly resourceful woman who is valued far beyond precious jewels, who makes home a retreat for her husband and children, whose light does not go out in loving care for her children, whose husband is given credibility because of her, who teaches kindness and a work ethic to her children, whose children call her blessed, and in whom is displayed the fear of the Lord.

The high calling of motherhood is something that the mother of John and Charles Wesley (great preachers of the gospel and hymn writers!) accepted readily. She is a great example to us. We cannot expect all mothers to give birth to 19 children as Susanna Wesley did, but it is in her acceptance of her highest calling that she committed herself to her role as mother. Acknowledging that the leadership responsibility of the family was her husband's, it was under his leadership that she cared for and instructed her children. She insisted on having an orderly home with structure and discipline, but also focused herself diligently on spending time with each of her many children individually to be a nurturing and truly loving role model in their lives. It is because of this dedication that both John and Charles Wesley gave their mother great acclaim and stated her as one of the major forces behind them going into ministry.

One of the attributes that is clearly explained in Susanna Wesley's own writings is her view of discipline and control in the home. Many have criticized Susanna Wesley for her strong stance of discipline in her home and even described it as harsh (and in some respects, I would agree). Yet she modeled her techniques on equipping her children to be God-honoring. Writing about developing the "will" of a child, she said:

> In order to firm the minds of children, the first thing to be done is to conquer their will and bring them to an obedient temper. To inform the understanding is a work of time, and must with children proceed by small degrees as they are able to bear it; but the subjecting the will is a thing that must be done at once, and the sooner the better, for by neglecting timely correction they will contract a stubbornness and obstinacy which are hardly ever after conquered, and never without using such severity as would be as painful to me as to the child. . . . And when the will of a child is totally subdued and it is brought to revere and stand in awe of the parents, then a great many childish follies and inadvertencies may be passed by. Some should be overlooked and taken no notice of, and others mildly reproved; but no willful transgression ought ever to be forgiven children without chastisement, less or more, as the nature and circumstances of the offence may require.[7]

This really is the value of a good mother. It complies with Scripture.

Whether we want to admit it or not, God gives parents instruction to discipline children, and God gives children the command to honor and obey parents. "He who spares his rod hates his son, but he who loves him disciplines him promptly" (Prov. 13:24). "Children, obey your parents in the Lord, for this is right. Honor your father and mother" (Eph. 6:1–2).

In Susanna Wesley I see a God-glorifying mother who has viewed her role as an essential and crucial high calling. Whether you have 1 child or 12, and whether you work or not, the values

---

7. Arnold. A Dallimore, *Susanna Wesley* (Grand Rapids, MI: Baker Book House, 1993), p. 60–61.

of care, nuture, provision, education, and godliness in Susanna Wesley are a great example to all moms. She helped her children understand the biblical expectation of obedience and honor to parents. She did this by obeying the Scriptures in relation to order and discipline in the home, and pouring out love and time into her children, with some great results. Her children were well-educated and well-disciplined; as she further describes: "Taking God's name in vain, cursing and swearing, profanity, obscenity, rude ill-bred names, were never heard among them."[8] Most of all, Susanna's main focus in motherhood was to see her children come to know Jesus as their Savior.

The world has given its own verdict to the questions facing women (and particularly mothers) today. The modern feminist movement has replaced motherhood with selfish ambition. The commercial world has seen both fathers and mothers replace their roles in raising children with simply providing them with things.

Possibly the most damaging philosophy imposed upon mothers and potential mothers is the one that says you can do whatever you like with your body. In a distorted pursuit of "women's rights" we have seen the very lives of children under threat and countless killings of innocent children through abortion. The distorted view of women's rights has become a destructive force against motherhood. How much more could the role of motherhood be undermined than for a woman to believe that the individually God-knitted baby conceived in her womb is part of her own body to do what she likes with?

The Bible, however, gives us the great example of a mother's protection and care for children that epitomizes true motherhood. We see a classic example of this in the account of the mother of Moses (Exod. 2:2–9):

> So the woman conceived and bore a son. And when she saw that he was a beautiful child, she hid him three months.

---

8. Ibid.

But when she could no longer hide him, she took an ark of bulrushes for him, daubed it with asphalt and pitch, put the child in it, and laid it in the reeds by the river's bank. And his sister stood afar off, to know what would be done to him.

Then the daughter of Pharaoh came down to bathe at the river. And her maidens walked along the riverside; and when she saw the ark among the reeds, she sent her maid to get it. And when she opened it, she saw the child, and behold, the baby wept. So she had compassion on him, and said, "This is one of the Hebrews' children."

Then his sister said to Pharaoh's daughter, "Shall I go and call a nurse for you from the Hebrew women, that she may nurse the child for you?"

And Pharaoh's daughter said to her, "Go." So the maiden went and called the child's mother. Then Pharaoh's daughter said to her, "Take this child away and nurse him for me, and I will give you your wages." So the woman took the child and nursed him.

It was clear that under the law of Pharaoh all newborn sons of Israelites were to be killed. How could a mother, a true mother, possibly do nothing about such an evil command from an earthly leader? God placed His future leader of Israel in the hands of a true mother who not only acted to save his life but put herself in a position to care for him. Mothers are called to protect children, not kill them.

When we look at the wonderful role of motherhood and how essential it is for raising godly offspring, it amazes me how many women see this role as something holding them back or somehow cramping their potential. I can only thank God that He placed me in the care of a lady who saw her role in motherhood as essential and primary. Mum was always there for me, nurturing me, encouraging me, and giving me godly instruction and advice under the leadership and teaching of my dad. My father's ministry was immensely more effective to both my family and others *because of my mother.*

This book is fundamentally about the authority of God and His Word. In many ways, the family is in a very poor position because we have denied the authority of God's Word and placed our own low value on motherhood. In many instances this has happened because men have not lived up to God's authoritative instructions for fatherhood.

TAKING BACK BIBLICAL INSTRUCTION

Proverbs 1:2–9 tells us two very important truths when it comes to parenting and imparting knowledge to children:

1. All true knowledge and wisdom come through the fear of the Lord.

2. This is the foundation for which parents are to instruct their children.

To know wisdom and instruction, to perceive the words of understanding, to receive the instruction of wisdom, justice, judgment, and equity; to give prudence to the simple, to the young man knowledge and discretion — a wise man will hear and increase learning, and a man of understanding will attain wise counsel, to understand a proverb and an enigma, the words of the wise and their riddles.

The fear of the Lord is the beginning of knowledge, but fools despise wisdom and instruction. My son, hear the instruction of your father, and do not forsake the law of your mother; for they will be a graceful ornament on your head, and chains about your neck.

We have already dealt with this issue to some degree in chapter 5 as we discussed axioms. As parents we must hold an axiomatic biblical authority when teaching and instructing in our homes or we ignore that the beginning of wisdom is truly the fear of the Lord.

The basis for teaching children is the Word of God. If God truly is the authority, His Word must be our first and foremost source of instruction for our children. This means not only the instruction in our homes but also in our choice of education and even in our choice of local church community, including Sunday school.

As we have previously found, there is no such thing as neutral education. In Australia, my children attended an independent evangelical Christian school. Even though we are generally pleased with our choice of education, we have also been at times disturbed by the secular philosophies creeping into our children's education. As parents we have had to pay much closer attention to what our children are learning and particularly how it might potentially influence their thinking. We do not believe that it is appropriate to abdicate our parental responsibilities to a school but to monitor and correct our children's education on the basis of the authority of Scripture. This has resulted in some discussions with the teachers at my children's school, and mostly (and thankfully) we have received gracious responses and a correction of the subject matter. In saying this, we have found on many occasions that our Christian school system still wanders into "supposed" neutrality rather than holding to biblical axioms. This has caused us to closely monitor and, as needed, correct what our children are being taught.

Children today live in a world that attempts to live and breathe neutrality. This is a neutrality that tells us that children must make up their own minds and that there is no place for biblical presuppositions in education. In other words, this is a world that is so ready to indoctrinate our children against Scripture that it will not allow for education to even consider biblical perspectives. Neutrality is a lie that has sadly started to creep into Christian schools and even into Christian families. I have even had Christian parents say to me that they are not going to aggressively promote Scripture to their children because they want them to make up their own minds. Sadly, this neutral position allows worldly philosophies to be the primary indoctrination of our children, and this is no different even in many of our

Christian schools. It is important that we see the idea of neutrality for what it really is. Making up one's own mind to follow one's own philosophical view is humanism. It is a false religion.

Often parents have an overly favorable view of their children. This is not a biblical position. Psalm 51:5 tells us that our children are sinful from conception. Proverbs 22:15 tells us that we require the rod of correction to deal with the foolishness in the hearts of our children. Ephesians 2:3 tells us that we are all (including adults) children of wrath. Our children do not have a built-in system of godly discernment in biblical truth. Unless we as parents teach our children how to view this world and discern through biblical axioms, our children *will* be influenced by the many deceiving philosophies of our time. Today there is none more deceiving than theories based on long ages and evolution that question the very authority of Scripture. Much of our modern education is based on it. Many people are happy to follow the thinking of the time, and depending on that thinking, this could be very good or very bad.

Dr. Louis Berkhof, who died in 1957 (when most of our parents and grandparents were enjoying a much stronger Christian influence in society), commented on the popular discernment in relation to authority and philosophical influence:

> Think of the tremendous influence exercised by such men as Plato and Aristotle, Augustine, and Thomas Aquinas, Luther and Calvin, Wesley and Jonathan Edwards, Kant and Hegel, Kuyper and Bavinck, most of whom have already dominated the thinking of centuries. The significance of this authority is enhanced by the fact that the great masses of the people do not think for themselves but allow others to do their thinking for them. The simple dictum of a great man is sufficient for them; they need no arguments. Hence it follows that this authority may be greatly abused; and history teaches us that it has often wrought havoc in the world.[9]

9. Louis Berkhoff and Cornelius Van Til, *Foundations of Christian Education* (Phillipsburg, NJ: Presbyterian and Reformed Publ. Co., 1990), p. 106.

This is an incredibly insightful comment from Berkhoff considering the popular opinion that Charles Darwin was a great man. It is very evident that his theory of evolution has had significant and devastating consequences in this world and continues to do so.

Regardless of what we do, our children will be indoctrinated. If we don't indoctrinate them with an axiom of biblical authority in our homes, Christian schools, and churches, the world will indoctrinate them with anti-God humanism. Parents have an overwhelming responsibility that cannot be abdicated to anyone else.

THE FIRST TASTE OF CHURCH

True Christian education is really biblical instruction. When God's Word is at the foundations of our worldview, and also all of our family values, discipline, instruction, and nurture, our families become our children's first taste of church. Our families are really to be mini-churches. The Church has become an irrelevant institution for many young people in the current generation, and much of this is because parents are not guiding their children in the realities of the Church at home, while at the same time children are being led to the religion of humanism through the school systems.

The family is where we get the first taste of life. For the Christian family, it is the first taste of life in Christ. Our children get to experience worship as we live together to honor and glorify God and reflect His image in our lives and to those around us. They get to experience the teaching of His Word and its application to the world around us and our very lives. They get to experience evangelism as we consistently teach and defend the gospel of Jesus. They get to experience Christian unity through the bond of Christ and His gospel. They get to understand the relevance of living under God's authority as the Word of God makes sense of the world. If biblically modeled, they also get to experience what it is to be under strong leadership and how to submit to that leadership as the entire family submits to Christ's headship. This is the great foretaste of Church. This *is* a church.

This also means that husbands and wives have a key ministry responsibility within their own family church. The husband has an oversight and pastoral role in the family and the wife is the great support in this role. R.C. Sproul Jr. edited a very practical little book about God's perspective for a healthy home. One of the contributors had this to say about the pastoral role of fathers:

> The duties of a Christian father are clear in Scripture, and they are pastoral in nature. This does not mean setting up a pulpit in the living room, or administering the sacraments around the dinner table. But a father is to bring up his children in the nurture and admonition of the Lord. A husband is to nourish and cherish his wife, loving her as Christ loved the church. These duties cannot be performed by anyone else in the church, and their performance (or lack of performance) directly affects the health of the church. Sound households are the key to a sound church.[10]

What is being suggested here is that healthy homes built solidly on the authority of the Word of God bring about healthy churches built on that same authority. This is a consistent teaching in Scripture. When God commanded the Israelite children to obey and honor their parents, He did so by promising that they would live long in the land He was giving them (Exod. 20:12). This was a reflection that a healthy family with obedient children would result in a healthy community in the Promised Land. As we read in Scripture, many of the laws of Moses apply to the family and impact the community. We read in Acts 16 two separate accounts of people who were converted along with their households, showing that God is interested in the whole family unit worshiping Him. What is even more astonishing is that there are a number of references in Scripture to people who had a church in their house (Rom. 16:5; Col.

---

10. R.C. Sproul Jr., editor, *Family Practice* (Phillipsburg, NJ: Presbyterian and Reformed Publ. Co., 2001), p. 88.

4:15). While these meetings may have consisted of more than the family unit, it is most certain that the family unit within the household was a central strength in the local church.

Maybe this is new to you and you are wondering how to help your children apply biblical teaching to their lives. I encourage you to revisit the list of materials in the appendix and use them to help your children establish a true biblical worldview. When your children see that the world makes sense to you because you see it through God's Word, it can also be an eye-opening experience of biblical relevance for them. Our children desperately need dads to lead them pastorally and moms to support them in this work as a strong, essential high calling. Biblical parental partnership is a powerful force for the Kingdom of God.

This all requires parents to first commit themselves to living for God and to come under the authority of His Word. Parents who are able to humble themselves and submit to God's model for the family, including taking on the responsibility for their roles as husbands and wives, will have the great blessing that comes with godly obedience. It is not a guarantee that your children will all follow the Lord. At the end of the day they will each be responsible to God individually. It is, however, a guarantee that they will have been thoroughly equipped to know the truth and be fully prepared for the world's attacks. Obedience to this training and especially in acceptance of the gospel is their own responsibility. This is why the parental pastoral prayer is essential. I know my mother and father prayed for me every day, and my mother continues to. Trish and I pray each day for Sarah and David. I praise God that both of my children have come to know and trust Him as Savior. I praise God that both of my children see through the lies of this world and often point out to me the folly of humanistic philosophy (especially evolutionary thinking). I praise God that He has used me to teach my family answers to defend His Word and make sense of this world. I praise Him for the reality and sure hope of His gospel for my family.

I pray that He may do the same for you. I pray that our families will not be a negative statistic. When it comes to taking back your family and creating strong hinges for your children, authority matters.

Chapter 12

Order in the House: Authority and the Church

For where God built a church, there the Devil would also build a chapel.[1] — Martin Luther

When Jesus ascended into heaven, He did not leave us without His authoritative presence. Acts 1:8 tells us that Jesus promised the Holy Spirit to be present in our lives and empower us to take His message to all ends of the earth. It was at this same time that the Church started to build. The Apostles and the rest of the disciples (including Jesus' mother and His brothers — see Acts 1:12) were charged with building the Church and spreading the gospel. Pentecost was the first great implementation of the Acts 1:8 promise, and the Holy Spirit, through the Apostles, catapulted the gospel into the languages of the modern world. And the Church, grounded in the gospel, began.

The Church has been building on the back of the Great Commission and Acts 1:8 ever since. The gospel of Jesus is the great platform of the Church and the message that Christ has empowered

1. www.en.wikiquote.org/wiki/Martin_Luther.

us to take to the nations. It is the single most important message for any man to hear because it is the only message in this world with eternal significance. Since the formation of the Church from the time of Christ's ascension, the Church has been the great witness of His death and Resurrection and continues to be the witness to this day.

With the Great Commission of the Church also comes great responsibility. There is only one gospel and therefore only one true Church. That Church is the people of God who have truly accepted Christ as Savior and Lord, and as the only way of salvation. The best way to decommission the Church is to undermine the gospel. The best way to undermine the gospel is to undermine the Word of God and to attack its messengers in the world. It is therefore true that Satan's great focus is an attack on the Church that takes this message to the world. He has attacked the Church on many fronts. He attacks our unity, he attacks our purity, he attacks our integrity, he attacks our message, and most of all he attacks God's truth and authority.

It is not surprising that Satan would attack the Church on as many fronts as possible, and yet God has given the Church His great and protective Word to keep us on His path of truth in this great spiritual war. Only upon the acceptance of God's authoritative Word, and a full reliance on the power and authority of the Holy Spirit in our lives, can the Church stand firm from Satan's attacks and also fulfill our duty in spreading Christ's gospel into this world. As we read God's Word, there are many Scriptures that show us that He has thoroughly equipped us with many tools for His Church to stay His course. The following is a list of some of the verses that give us an insight into the roles and functions of the Church that are in addition to the Church's great calling in the Great Commission. Within this list we will expand upon three of these functions over which many in the modern Church have lost their way.

1. **Order and organization (1 Cor. 14:33):** *For God is not the author of confusion but of peace, as in all the churches of the saints.*

2. **Edification (Heb. 10:24–25):** *And let us consider one another in order to stir up love and good works, not forsaking the assembling of ourselves together, as is the manner of some, but exhorting one another, and so much the more as you see the Day approaching.*

3. **Teaching (Acts 2:42):** *And they continued steadfastly in the apostles' doctrine and fellowship, in the breaking of bread, and in prayers.*

4. **Service (Heb. 6:10):** *For God is not unjust to forget your work and labor of love which you have shown toward His name, in that you have ministered to the saints, and do minister.*

5. **Leadership and governance (Acts 20:28):** *Therefore take heed to yourselves and to all the flock, among which the Holy Spirit has made you overseers, to shepherd the church of God which He purchased with His own blood.*

6. **Protecting and proclaiming good doctrine (Titus 1:9):** *Holding fast the faithful word as he has been taught, that he may be able, by sound doctrine, both to exhort and convict those who contradict.*

7. **Sacraments for remembrance (Acts 2:42):** *And they continued steadfastly in the apostles' doctrine and fellowship, in the breaking of bread, and in prayers.*

8. **Discipline and correction (Titus 3:10–11):** *Reject a divisive man after the first and second admonition, knowing that such a person is warped and sinning, being self-condemned.*

9. **Fellowship of love and forgiveness (Col. 3:13):** *Bearing with one another, and forgiving one another, if anyone has a complaint against another; even as Christ forgave you, so you also must do.*

10. **A community to help the fallen (James 5:16):** *Confess your trespasses to one another, and pray for one another, that you may be healed. The effective, fervent prayer of a righteous man avails much.*

11. **A community to support those suffering under satanic attack (1 Pet. 5:8–9):** *Be sober, be vigilant; because your adversary the devil walks about like a roaring lion, seeking whom he may devour. Resist him, steadfast in the faith, knowing that the same sufferings are experienced by your brotherhood in the world.*

12. **A church that is both universal (invisible) and local (visible) (1 Cor. 1:2):** *To the church of God which is at Corinth, to those who are sanctified in Christ Jesus, called to be saints, with all who in every place call on the name of Jesus Christ our Lord, both theirs and ours.*

13. **A Church with a truly hopeful future (Titus 2:11–13):** *For the grace of God that brings salvation has appeared to all men, teaching us that, denying ungodliness and worldly lusts, we should live soberly, righteously, and godly in the present age, looking for the blessed hope and glorious appearing of our great God and Savior Jesus Christ.*

14. **A Church who will reign in victory (2 Tim. 4:8):** *Finally, there is laid up for me the crown of righteousness, which the Lord, the righteous Judge, will give to me on that Day, and not to me only but also to all who have loved His appearing.*

This is God's true Church, and as we peruse those 14 Scriptures we are able to look around us and gauge how we are doing. We are not a perfect Church and we do let ourselves down in relation to many of these required attributes. Sometimes we do not do well in protecting doctrine and we allow the gospel to be undermined. Sometimes we place culture and community above God's truth and authority. Sometimes we allow sin to reign within the Church because we have been too weak to discipline in leadership. Sometimes we have hurt the Church because we have not been prepared to forgive or reconcile. We could go on and on considering these wonderful attributes of God's Church, and it is a productive exercise (especially for pastors and elders) to ponder how we see these attributes in our own local churches. For now we must consider where the Church is most being undermined (or attacked) in relation to the acceptance of God's authority in our present world.

Today the Church in the world has become somewhat more visible. We live in an age where everything has become instantaneous. If we want to say something about someone for all to see, today we have the most amazing tool to do it with — the Internet. It is through the Internet that the best and worst of the world is on display, immediately available, and nonretractable. I have certainly seen the Internet used in a most deceitful and malicious way to discredit the good name and character of good people. The Internet has become the fastest game of telephone whispers ever played on earth, and once the spread of even a single piece of information has reached thousands or even millions of sources, it can never be retrieved. I have been able to Google a single comment by a well-known pastor and obtain dozens of possible avenues to read the interpretations of people I will never meet who now through the Internet have a global voice. Unfortunately, with millions of global voices also come millions of fallible, sinful opinions that lead to misrepresentations. Nevertheless, the Internet has also been used for good and has allowed access to some wonderful materials from some very godly people indeed. Most churches now have websites where we can download sermons, schedule events, read the statement of faith, and under-stand the local church's stand on the Word of God.

It is through an even more visible Church that we have seen the modern culture of our day have its influence. There are churches that have withstood the philosophies of our time to stand on the authority of God's Word, but sadly, many churches to varying degrees have allowed cultural influence to compromise God's design for the Church. The culture around us today has influenced many in relation to its postmodern thinking as it rejects the idea of ulti-mate authority. We have seen this response in movements such as the emergent church, which has based gospel belief on a discussion of opinions rather than biblical truth. We have seen feminist move-ments influence the Church with a misguided sense of equality com-promising the biblical model of Church governance and leadership. We have also seen a culture in opposition to the concept of judgment apply pressure within the Church on communicating and correcting according to God's judgment on sin. This, to some degree, has influ-enced the Church in taking a soft approach on sin, discipline, and correction within the Church in the name of not being judgmental. There have certainly been churches that have all but lost discipline and correction in place of a misinterpreted grace, love, and accep-tance. We should therefore look closely into these few issues where it is truly time for the Church to take back our submission to God's authority over the culture we live in. This does not mean we should not be culturally relevant in our approach to saving others, but at no time are we to compromise the truth of God's Word or our obedi-ence to it. The Christian Church should already believe and accept that God's Word is relevant for every generation . . . *and it is.*

PROTECTING AND PROCLAIMING GOOD DOCTRINE

Many have argued that maintaining a strongly held (dogmatic) biblical stance is culturally irrelevant. Naturally, God disagrees with this view in His Word. It is unfortunate that many who are calling themselves Christians have felt the need to meet a post-modern culture by questioning such truths as the virgin birth or the Resurrection of Christ. This has been particularly visible within the "emergent church" and has gained some significant momentum through its many very public mouthpieces. The good intentions of the emergent church were to reach a culture that has become disengaged with the Church. However, the compromise position in doing this has resulted in a gospel that is no longer a gospel. It is interesting to note that one pastor who was once much closer to this movement has distanced himself to preserve and defend the essential elements of the gospel message. He now states:

> What I am arguing for is a two-handed approach to Christian ministry. In our firmly closed hand we must hold the timeless truths of Christianity, such as the solas of the reformation. In our graciously open hand we must hold the timely ministry methods and styles that adapt as the cultures and subcultures we are ministering to change. . . . I am not arguing for relativism, by which truth is abandoned and all of life and doctrine is lived out of an open hand. Rather, I am arguing for relevantism, by which doctrinal principles remain in a closed hand and cultural methods remain in an open hand.[2]

This pastor has argued that the approach to our community is not the issue compared to the doctrine that we must abide by in the Church. If we do not hold that doctrine closely and protect it, we attempt to reach a community with an impotent message of no use or purpose.[3]

---

2. John Piper and Justin Taylor, general editors, *The Supremacy of Christ in a Postmodern World* (Westchester, IL: Crossway Books, 2007), p. 143.

3. It should be noted that while holding to the necessity of a closed hand for doctrine (of which I applaud), both Driscoll and Piper have allowed the influence of millions of years into their teaching when it comes to the authority of the Bible in Genesis. However, this can also be said in relation to a couple of other quoted authors highlighting the need for discernment. Many strong evangelical Christian leaders would also say that Driscoll and Piper's open hands of cultural relevantism are a little too open.

It is therefore of the utmost importance that the Church stand firmly on the doctrines of faith that are deemed essential for church unity and foundational for gospel understanding. One of my favorite little books that I revisit regularly is by one of my preaching heroes, Dr. D.M. Lloyd-Jones, and his book is called *What Is an Evangelical?* In discussing evangelicalism, Dr. Lloyd-Jones stated that there are some foundational truths that must be maintained and are essential for true Christian unity. He outlines some of these in particular, including *Scripture — the only and full authority; creation — not evolution; the Fall and evil; and one way of salvation.* Within these he also describes the doctrine of the Trinity, the Second Coming, understanding salvation, an acceptance of the virgin birth, and the Resurrection of Christ.[4]

There are two main attacks on Christian doctrine today: (1) the deity (exaltation) of Jesus Christ and salvation only through Him, and (2) the authority of Scripture (particularly in respect to creation).

Without being able to defend the authority of Scripture, the Church is impotent in defending Jesus and any moral living issues that are a part of following Christ in obedience. One of the reasons people are questioning the virgin birth or even the Resurrection of Christ is because such miracles have no scientific proof. In addition, historical scientific belief in evolutionary or long-age theory has been accepted by many in the Church. This belief has as its presupposition an opposition to the straightforward reading of the Genesis account of creation, and those proposing have also been required to doubt a straightforward reading of the account of the virgin birth or the Resurrection. People have not yet understood that an attack upon Genesis truly is an effectual attack on Jesus. In Psalm 11:3 we read, *"If the foundations are destroyed, what can the righteous do?"* The key reason my brother Ken, Dr. Morris, Dr. Whitcomb, and others went into ministry to defend Genesis was not with an end aim of defending creationism but with an end aim of defending and proclaiming

4. D.M. Lloyd-Jones, *What Is an Evangelical?* (Edinburgh, UK: Banner of Truth, 1992), section 3.

the gospel of Jesus Christ. The Church is losing ground in this area. Starting in our own little family house churches, we must hold true to the foundational doctrines of the authority of Scripture. We need to understand that the philosophy of our time that most attempts to undermine the authority of Scripture (and therefore the reliability of the gospel) is the belief of evolution and long ages.

In his travels, Ken has seen the devastating effect that the acceptance of the models of evolution (even partially) has had on the Church and is the reason he wrote his book *The Lie: Evolution*. In it he states:

> In Western nations most churches compromise with evolution. Many theological and Bible colleges teach that the issue of creation/evolution does not matter. They teach that you can believe in both evolution and the Bible because you do not have to bother about taking Genesis literally. This compromising stand is helping to destroy the very structure they claim to want to remain in society — the structure of Christianity.[5]

This is also where we must revisit the truth of the authority of the Holy Spirit. When the Church compromises biblical authority to modernize a message or make it culturally acceptable, we deny our acceptance of the Holy Spirit's authority to work His authentic message in the hearts of men. If you study any of the great historic revivals you will note an unwavering acceptance in the heart of the preachers of the authority of Scripture.

In his book on the study of revival, Brian Edwards has recognized this common trait in preachers prior to the beginning of a great revival:

> Long before Lloyd-Jones or North or Spurgeon — Peter Waldo in the twelfth century, John Wycliffe in the fourteenth, Edwards, Whitefield and Wesley in the eighteenth,

5. Ken Ham, *The Lie: Evolution* (Green Forest, AR: Master Books, 1987), p. 111.

and a host of others, who were all leaders in times of revival, were fully committed to the authority of the Bible. And they were equally committed to obedience to it. They did not preach what they did not believe, and they did not believe what they did not obey.[6]

Through the ages the Church has never had to reject issues related to cultural relevance, and we certainly do not have to now. We can embrace various forms of multimedia, different music styles (as long as there is room for the edification of all ages), and even diverse building styles. We must, however, hold tightly to uncompromising essential doctrines:

1. the full and sole authority of Scripture
2. the doctrine of God: the Trinity
3. creation (not evolution)
4. the doctrine of sin and judgment
5. the doctrine of the Son and one way to salvation
6. the Second Coming and consummation of all things

We may and should hold other doctrines such as eschatology or doctrines of election or human responsibility. But these we must hold with a loose hand for the sake of unity. We must not, however, uphold unity over the truth of those doctrines essential to either the foundational understanding of the gospel (understanding of the reason for or reliability of the gospel) or particularly those that have an impact on the saving understanding of the gospel of Christ (elements of the gospel message essential for salvation). Many men who have upheld biblical authority and held fast to essential doctrine have been used by God in bringing a revival upon His Church.

THE BIBLICAL MODEL FOR LEADERSHIP AND GOVERNANCE

My family gets itself into lots of trouble. My father was a man who was loved or hated (unfortunately, sometimes even within the

---

6. Brian Edwards, *Revival: A People Saturated with God* (Darlington, UK: Evangelical Press, 1990), p. 67.

church). My brothers and I get the same treatment, especially Ken. I suppose it is because we see that the Bible teaches that we are either for God or against Him. Sometimes we take biblical positions that simply make this world mad. It's because none of us can see any sense in accepting that God is truly God without accepting that He (and not us) is the authority. What really is the point of worshiping a God who is the omniscient Creator and then disagreeing with Him on the basis of some human philosophy?

There are many people, including clergy, who simply don't want to accept God's authority as genuine or complete. Many attempt to take God's authority as a partial view and adapt man's authority when it is more convenient or popular to do so. The questions we need to ask ourselves are: Is God omnipotent or not? Is God omniscient or not? Either God is the authority over everything or He's not at all. When it comes to the acceptance of God's authority, the Bible does not leave a middle ground for humans to pick the subjects they want to be master of.

Biblical leadership is one of those areas where many churches have adopted a human authority over God. There is no topic more touchy than discussing God's model for Church leadership, and yet under His authority I am satisfied to be loved or hated. This is emotive probably because one cannot consider this issue without the consideration of the roles of men and women in the Church. On this one, despite feminist, cultural, or even majority pressure — I answer to God.

We have seen that a compromise to adapt to postmodern culture in the emergent church certainly resulted in a breakdown of the authentic gospel message. In the same way, many churches have given way for the acceptance of influence from the modern feminist movement. They have adopted liberal theology to promote what they believe is a culturally acceptable leadership. Some have used unique and often obscure interpretations of Scripture to assert that the Bible teaches that Church governance and spiritual oversight positions of pastors and elders are open to both men and women.

Before I discuss this, I must clear one thing up very quickly. This discussion is not about values or equality but about roles and God's design for Church governance. We have misinterpreted this issue because in our society we have been deceived into thinking that submission equals lesser value. This is not a biblical concept. Look carefully at what Paul writes to the Galatians.

> For you are all sons of God through faith in Christ Jesus. For as many of you as were baptized into Christ have put on Christ. There is neither Jew nor Greek, there is neither slave nor free, there is neither male nor female; for you are all one in Christ Jesus. And if you are Christ's, then you are Abraham's seed, and heirs according to the promise (Gal. 3:26–29).

A slave on this earth is certainly submissive to his master or employer. (Note: slavery under Old Testament law should also be differentiated from the harsh type of slavery of the Egyptians or even the European history of slavery in the last 500 years. It was more like a bondservant/bankruptcy law.) There is no expression of submission in one who is free. In the modern-day context, I have been the free person. I have had employees in my business and they have reported to me. You could definitely say that they were submissive to me. But Paul is saying that in Christ, whether in a submission or leadership role on this earth, there is no difference in value or equality. If we belong to Christ we are equally heirs with Him for eternity. Slavery or freedom, gender, or earthly birthright matter not to God when it comes to salvation. Roles of submission and leadership have nothing to do with value or equality.

Unfortunately, many have misinterpreted Scripture on the basis of worldly standards and believe that it is placing a lower value on women to suggest that they are not candidates for spiritual oversight positions of elder or overseer in a church. (When the Bible talks of these positions we sometimes read it translated as elder, overseer, or even bishop. For the purpose of this discussion I will name the role as elder.) It is not just a distinction between men and women that Scripture makes in relation to these positions. If we read through the qualification of elders in 1 Timothy and Titus we read that God has ordained this role to only a select group of men with specific qualifications:

> This is a faithful saying: If a man desires the position of a bishop, he desires a good work. A bishop then must be blameless, the husband of one wife, temperate, sober-minded, of good behavior, hospitable, able to teach; not given to wine, not violent, not greedy for money, but gentle, not quarrelsome, not covetous; one who rules his own house well, having his children in submission with all reverence (for if a man does not know how to rule his own house, how will he take care of the church of God?); not a novice, lest being puffed up with pride he fall into the same condemnation as the devil. Moreover he must have a good testimony among those who are outside, lest he fall into reproach and the snare of the devil (1 Tim. 3:1–7).

I normally find that this does not open the door to all men but only a very few men in the Church.

It is not appropriate to say that women are to submit to every man the same way a wife is to submit to her husband or Church members are to submit to leadership. The Bible's position is clear. Children are to submit to parents; wives are to submit to husbands; and men, women, and children are to submit to the few men ordained to lead in spiritual oversight in the Church. All are to submit to Christ. Not all men are called to be elders, and these men who are not elders are to be just as submissive to Church leadership as every woman in the Church. In saying this, I believe the biblical position from the point of creation is that men are to generally care for and protect women and provide good leadership.

Within the realms of the Church body and even in the family unit, we are also all called to general submission toward each other.

"Speaking to one another in psalms and hymns and spiritual songs, singing and making melody in your heart to the Lord, giving thanks always for all things to God the Father in the name of our Lord Jesus Christ, submitting to one another in the fear of God" (Eph. 5:19–21). If we need more proof that submission does not equate to value, we have one major text. "He went a little farther and fell on His face, and prayed, saying, 'O My Father, if it is possible, let this cup pass from Me; nevertheless, not as I will, but as You will' " (Matt. 26:39). In Jesus we see God the Son, fully man and yet fully God, and we see Him submissive to the Father. Yet we know that He and the Father are one. Submission requires a godliness that Christ Himself exhibited.

We only have a problem with submission because our pride and this sinful world demand it. For the Christian, however, submission is a godly pursuit. This is a pursuit that we are all undertaking for each other in a general sense. In a specific sense, wives are given this pursuit of submission in relation to their husbands, and men and women are given this pursuit in relation to the few men chosen to be elders in the Church.

I have spent time on this area of submission because I believe it to be a word that has been widely misrepresented in many churches. It is through this misrepresentation that I have also come to great concern in relation to motherhood. It is certainly true that the unfortunate picture of a mother in Australian society has been that of a woman who is barefoot and pregnant with her hands tied to the sink and children latching on to the hem of her dress. This is also an incorrect picture of submission. In the last chapter we discussed that biblical motherhood is different from this. It is a wide-ranging, diverse, crucial, and essential high calling for many women. To suggest that women do not achieve their potential if they cannot fulfill the role of elder is to understate the role of motherhood. This is why Paul wrote to Timothy and emphasized that women were not to be given for eldership but to be preserved (or saved) for motherhood. "Nevertheless she will be saved in child-bearing if they continue in faith, love, and holiness, with self-control" (1 Tim. 2:15).

The Church, in accepting God's authority for leadership, will be a training ground for building men of quality who can fulfill eldership roles. It will also be a training ground for women of quality who can raise the next generation of leaders, women like Susanna Wesley.

We have sadly dropped the ball in many of our churches and have not consistently trained our men and women appropriately, blurring the roles that God has ordained. From *Life in the Father's House*:

> Unfortunately, as in the area of leadership, there is often a lack of men willing and able to fulfill this role [teaching], and that sad fact has contributed to the growing number of women in teaching positions. If churches want to stem the tide of this reversal of biblical roles, it will not be enough simply to emphasize the restrictions placed on women in ministry — they will also have to emphasize the need for men to develop their teaching abilities.[7]

This is one of many reasons why the Church needs to be a training ground to help men not only teach true and correct doctrine based on biblical authority in their families but also to develop them for congregational leadership in God's Word.

The blurring of roles in the churches has led to far worse consequences. It has led to the acceptance of homosexual lifestyles and even homosexual clergy. It has also led to a warped view of God as "mother," and inconsistent teachings about Jesus. It has even led to a feminization of Scripture, and in this vein a re-translation of the Bible (TNIV) for the purpose of simply having a more gender-neutral translation. It has led to a devaluation of motherhood (which to me is incredibly sad) and an apathetic group of men, untrained to

---

7. Wayne A. Mack and Dave Swavely, *Life in the Father's House: A Members' Guide to the Local Church* (Phillipsburg, NJ: P&R Publ., 2006), p. 100.

be real men and unwilling to step up and lead. Lastly, the blurring of roles in the Church is linked closely to liberal theology.

The history of the ordination of women in Protestant churches in the United States has been assessed through a sociological study (by Mark Chaves) published by Harvard University Press. About this study, Wayne Grudem comments:

> Quite a clear connection between theological liberalism and the endorsement of women's ordination. . . . From Chave's study we can observe a pattern among the mainstream Protestant denominations whose leadership is dominated by theological liberals (that is, those who reject the idea that the entire Bible is the written word of God, and is therefore truthful in all it affirms).[8]

In other words, where theological liberalism reigns, so does women's ordination.

In accepting biblical authority, it is time for the Church to take back biblical eldership, lead God's people, and raise the next godly generation.

CORRECTION AND DISCIPLINE

We should touch upon this subject in relation to authority and Church correction and discipline. The Church is often willing to claim biblical authority, but exercising biblical authority is often another matter, as John MacArthur notes:

> People have asked me, "Why is the church in America, even the evangelical church, so unholy?" The issue isn't necessarily that we have preached the wrong message but that we have neglected its implementation in the lives of people. We have told them, in effect, "As long as you hear a doctrinally correct sermon, we really don't care how you live." But you can't rear children in such extreme permissiveness that

---

8. Wayne Grudem, *Evangelical Feminism and Biblical Truth* (Sisters, OR: Multnomah Publishers, 2004), p. 500.

resorts only to reasoning with them. I would hate to spend a day with your children if, all their lives, you had merely told them what to do but never disciplined them![9]

MacArthur's statement is a simple and yet profound insight into the modern Church. I believe most of us could consider times in our own churches where we would agree that a person or persons should have come under the active correction of the Church but didn't. Even in our own lives, a supportive and corrective action from a godly Christian would have been helpful. I can certainly admit that I have at times benefited from the corrective words from a Christian brother or sister in Christ.

In many of Paul's letters we see the pen of correction. In writing to Timothy, Paul instructs him on how to correct the false teaching that has crept into the church of Ephesus. He also talks of dealing with the perpetrators. In writing to the Corinthians, Paul is dealing with not only wrongful teaching but also the actions of the church at Corinth as they had compromised their stance on Scripture for overtly sinful influences among them. It is at this letter that we must have a closer look.

There is no doubt that Paul is speaking to Christians, because in many places in the first letter to the Corinthians he calls them brothers. He also talks of them being called by God, being saints, and being people who have been given the grace of Jesus (1 Cor. 1:1–4). These "saints" were living in a city that was known for explicit sexual sin mixed with a full menu of false gods and religious beliefs. It was an environment of godless self-indulgence, and to some degree the local church had allowed this influence into the Church. The whole first letter to the Corinthians has Paul calling the church into order and back to God's true calling on their lives and doing so through straightening correction and, in at least one instance (chapter 5), insisting on strong disciplinary action.

---

9. John MacArthur, *The Master's Plan for the Church* (Chicago, IL: Moody Press, 1991), p. 265.

Paul makes a profound statement about the nature of the church:

> And I, brethren, could not speak to you as to spiritual people but as to carnal, as to babes in Christ. I fed you with milk and not with solid food; for until now you were not able to receive it, and even now you are still not able; for you are still carnal. For where there are envy, strife, and divisions among you, are you not carnal and behaving like mere men? (1 Cor. 3:1–3).

Paul is making his point that while the Corinthian church continues to behave carnally, they are not taking their relationship with God seriously. They are like infants. They are, as John MacArthur stated, like undisciplined children. If you read through the remainder of this letter from Paul, you will find that he is consistently correcting the behavior of this church. They were going beyond Scripture in their teaching and practices, they were not differentiated from the sinful society about them, they had no strong men stepping up in leadership, they had allowed perverse sexual lifestyle into the church without discipline, they were having lawsuits against each other, they were not holding a high view of marriage, they were not dealing with idolatry in their midst, they were defiling the Lord's supper, they were being sinfully indulgent rather than sharing in unity, they were placing themselves in front of order and edification in the Church, and they were being apathetic in proclaiming the risen Christ because they were caught up with the cultural infiltration among them.

If the Church is truly accepting the authority of God's Word, we must also be presenting ourselves in obedience to His Word. Disobedience is not acceptable to God, and the devastation and judgment of sin is a constant reminder to us all. We are all prone to sin and therefore must all be prone to correction. In saying this, even in churches that preach the doctrine of sin and judgment, many studies show few are willing to take truly practical correction measures within the congregation. I am not advocating that we all walk around as policemen looking for our brothers' or sisters' sin. We are all sinners. The biblical position, however, is that we are all prepared to deal with sin in our midst in a way that supports the sinner to reconcile first with the Lord and then with those who have been sinned against. The Church that truly deals with sin in the gracious and biblical manner should be a safe place for all believers and a welcoming place for those outside the faith. The Bible gives us plenty of good guidance in dealing with conflict and sin in our midst. Matthew 18–19 is a great place to start. The whole Church of believers is responsible for the correction process in the Church. One of the reasons that Paul was writing to the Corinthians is because the Church did not take on the responsibility of dealing with the issues themselves.

It is also true that sometimes a person not willing to repent and deal with his sin appropriately must be disciplined. Many churches would likely stop short of ever carrying this through, but in the spirit of protecting the holiness in the Church, Paul clearly instructs the Corinthians to carry out discipline. This is not only for the sake of the Church, however, but also for the sinner to come under God's judgment and perhaps be brought to repentance and reconciliation.

> I wrote to you in my epistle not to keep company with sexually immoral people. Yet I certainly did not mean with the sexually immoral people of this world, or with the covetous, or extortioners, or idolaters, since then you would need to go out of the world. But now I have written to you not to keep company with anyone named a brother, who is sexually immoral, or covetous, or an idolater, or a reviler, or a drunkard, or an extortioner — not even to eat with such a person. For what have I to do with judging those also who are outside? Do you not judge those who are inside? But those who are outside God judges. Therefore "put away from yourselves the evil person" (1 Cor. 5:9–13).

Some people read these statements and are shocked that the Church might even contemplate "putting someone out" of the Church. Paul is basically telling the Church that we have two choices: (1) leave the unrepentant brother or sister in our midst, allowing the sin to continue without consequence and make no differentiation to the world, or (2) put the unrepentant brother or sister out and seek for that person to be reconciled to God while you commit to seeking God's holiness in unity.

How is the Church to differentiate itself if we are telling the community around us that it is perfectly okay to slander your brother or take them to court or live in a sexually immoral lifestyle whether you are in or out of the Church body? Sin is destructive, and it appears that the modern Church still does not understand the concept that we live constantly with sin at our door. How are we to remain strong in faith and obedience if we are not willing to help each other appropriately deal with sin? The Church should be one place where we can truly help each other deal with sin for the constant reconciliation between God and us for the unity of His people, and to obey His command in becoming salt and light in this world.

It is possible that there are some churches that may be willing to follow through with church discipline in a situation of an overt sexual nature. For as many that do, there are churches that have embraced immoral relationships into membership or even into the clergy. As has happened in many countries, a major denomination in Australia has introduced the ordination of homosexual men and women into the church. Even though sexual immorality is still a problem within the Church and will continue to be while we remain in this world, there is another problem in the modern Church that has become a major phenomena. Books such as *The Wounded Minister* by Guy Greenfield, *Character Assassins* by Peter Hammond, and *Clergy Killers* by G. Lloyd Rediger have studied the effect of pathological antagonists within congregations and in the parachurch environment.

James 3:6–10 really says it all:

And the tongue is a fire, a world of iniquity. The tongue is so set among our members that it defiles the whole body, and sets on fire the course of nature; and it is set on fire by hell. For every kind of beast and bird, of reptile and creature of the sea, is tamed and has been tamed by mankind. But no man can tame the tongue. It is an unruly evil, full of deadly poison. With it we bless our God and Father, and with it we curse men, who have been made in the similitude of God. Out of the same mouth proceed blessing and cursing. My brethren, these things ought not to be so.

Sadly, the ministry of malice has become a growing trend in churches and has become a destructive influence. Only with the strongest biblically qualified elders committed to scriptural application can a church overcome the destructive nature of a pathological antagonist. In Australia, we call it the tall poppy syndrome. When someone is in authority over us or becomes successful in some way, sadly, Australian culture loves to see them fall off their pedestal. It should not be a surprise to us that people with public ministries of teaching God's truth would be not only unpopular but also subject to malicious attack. Peter Hammond describes it this way in *Character Assassins*:

Pride often is the engine which drives the gossip industry. It is a desire to portray people better than us in a bad light, to lift ourselves up by pulling others down. "Therefore rid yourselves of all malice and deceit, hypocrisy, envy and slander of every kind" (1 Peter 2:1). Slander is inextricably linked with malice, deceit, hypocrisy, and envy.[10]

Sadly, I have witnessed this kind of behavior, which included not only the public denigration of a man's character (by a fellow

---

10. Peter Hammond, Brian Abshire, and Bill Bathman, *Character Assassins* (Capetown, South Africa: Christian Liberty Books, 2004), p. 27.

Christian) but also actions of lawsuits against him. It remains undisciplined in the Church today.

We should always remember that Satan hates the Church with a passion. He hates God. But Satan also trembles under the coming judgment of Christ. The Church has all that it needs in the power of God and His Word to stand firm against Satan's attacks. Standing on the authority of God's Word by protecting His doctrine, providing biblically based leadership, and being prepared to correct and even discipline sinful behavior will keep the Church strong until He comes.

It is in this strength that the Church can best fulfill its greatest commission in Matthew 28:19–20 — to be the servants of God as He reaches His lost sheep in this world. This will be the focus of our final chapter.

Chapter 13

Tell the Nations: Authority and the Mission of the Gospel

Go therefore and make disciples of all the nations, baptizing them in the name of the Father and of the Son and of the Holy Spirit. — The Lord Jesus (Matt. 28:19)

If you have men who will only come if they know there is a good road, I don't want them. I want men who will come if there is no road at all.[1] — David Livingstone

In 1997 Trish and I were privileged to be able to travel to Africa in what we often describe as one of the most amazing experiences of our lifetimes. From the rich African culture to the spectacular scenery and, of course, the amazing diversity of animal and bird life, we were constantly left with our mouths wide open.

During this adventure we participated in a canoe trip down the Zambezi River bordering Zimbabwe and Zambia. Unconfidently paddling, we constantly kept a watch out for the dangerous hippos and attempted to enjoy the scenery. It wasn't too hard to imagine

---

1. www.brainyquote.com/quotes/authors/d/david_livingstone.html.

the cautious excitement that might have been building in David Livingstone over 150 years earlier as he also canoed on that very same part of the river toward the place the Africans called the *Smoke that Thunders*: Victoria Falls.

Livingstone is well-known for many things. He is known for opening Africa to the world and being the first European to see Victoria Falls, he wrote much on the geology of Africa, and, most famously, he is known for planting the gospel as a missionary for Jesus. While it seems from Livingstone's own writings there were only a few converts to Christ through his direct ministry, the work completed by Dr. Livingstone opened the way for a great many that followed him, and the work of the gospel in Africa escalated rapidly from that point.

Livingstone was also most certainly a man with great courage. He often faced death at the hands of the African tribes. He was also once mauled by a lion and always lived under the banner of venturing into the unknown. In all this, his most dearly held Scripture was from Matthew 28:20: "*And lo, I am with you always, even to the end of the age.*" It is not insignificant that Livingstone chose a verse communicated by Jesus immediately after giving the Great Commission. Like many other missionaries of the gospel, David Livingstone acknowledged that the gospel is not only the most important message this world needs to know, but also that God will not forsake us in being His servants delivering His message. David Livingstone died on the mission field, having established a basis for other missionaries to follow him. The Lord certainly blessed this ministry with an ongoing delivery of His gospel message to Africa through many people who have since accepted the mission to go. If the missionaries who followed Livingstone were traveling to Africa with the same mentality, they went knowing that the road of mission work was not an easy one. Anyone looking for an easy road was not appropriately understanding the mission of the gospel.

With great courage and a strong sense of peace in God, David Livingstone was prepared to go not where there were "good (or easy) roads" but to where there were no roads at all. Yet for the courage and great work completed by David Livingstone, he also allowed the philosophies of his time to impact his own belief. One is left to wonder if his ministry might have been even more impacting if he had been able to communicate from a more authoritative position.

David Livingstone was certainly not a naturalist. He truly did believe that God was Creator and that all life is attributable to God:

> When one looks at the wonderful adaptations through-out creation, and the varied operations carried on with such wisdom and skill, the idea of second causes looks clumsy. We are viewing the direct handiwork of Him who is the one and only Power in the universe; wonderful in counsel; in whom we all live, and move, and have our being.[2]

He finished his book in 1857, two years before the release of Darwin's *Origin of the Species* and 14 years prior to *The Descent of Man*, also authored by Darwin. Yet the idea of long ages in relation to geology had been around for some time prior to Darwin (also influencing Darwin) from people such as geologists Charles Lyell and Roderick Murchison, who presupposed long ages in their own philosophy in the early 1800s. David Livingstone was particularly influenced by the writings of Roderick Murchison, and it appeared to have had an impact on how he would then view God's grace to man through Christ:

> So far from this science having any tendency to make men undervalue the power or love of God, it leads to the probability that the exhibition of mercy we have in the gift of his Son may possibly not be the only manifestation of grace which has taken place in the countless ages during which works of creation have *been going on*[3] (emphasis added).

---

2. David Livingstone, *Missionary Travels and Researches in South Africa*, February 11, 2006, www.gutenberg.org/files/1039/1039.txt.
3. Ibid.

It is unclear what Dr. Livingstone really meant by the gift of Jesus not being the only manifestation of God's grace as he applies a theory of "countless ages" of creation. It is, however, very clear in the Bible that there is only one gift of salvation and it is only given to human beings through Christ, who determined this even before the first act of creation.

In Livingstone's time, as he witnessed to an African people who had never been influenced by long age views and especially not the belief of evolution, the major barriers to faith were pagan culture and tradition. No doubt these were huge barriers in themselves, and he describes having enormous difficulty in overcoming cultural traditions that were anything but godly. They included such traditions as killing any infant who developed their first teeth from the top jaw and proving manhood through polygamy.

It is also unknown as to what impact his writing on geology had upon his actual communication of the gospel, yet reading through his discussions one ascertains quickly that he had not considered the environment around him from a biblical axiom and omitted to consider the great devastation of Noah's Flood, especially in one instance where he attempts to discuss *"(sea) shells found in the carboniferous limestone (in an inland quarry)."*[4] He had no biblical answers as to why there might be seashells in an inland quarry. If Livingstone were alive today, he might say that seashells in quarries had no bearing on conversations with African people of the time. I would debate that (given that the problems culture was facing are explained through the understanding of a literal Genesis 1–11). But even if he were right, would Livingstone's long age presuppositions have allowed him to preach a gospel with authority to an evolutionized culture today? Even so, the African people Livingstone was preaching to had no concept of the need for a Savior and couldn't have without understanding of a perfect creation from a perfect God and the corruption of sin and God's judgment. One wonders after reading some of Livingstone's

4. Ibid.

statements if he was teaching a foundational understanding to the gospel he was preaching.

What may have had little impact in Livingstone's day, and in the culture in which he was an evangelist, is now in our culture one of the foremost reasons why people are unwilling to listen to the message of Christ. A compromise with either long age or evolutionary principles has caused many to doubt the authority and relevance of the Scriptures. Sadly, many Christians are, in action (if not also in belief), questioning the authority of the Bible that they themselves attest to. Instead of first considering evidence from the straightforward reading of Scripture, many are immediately compromising with belief systems that at their core attempt to deny God. In other words, because of the majority belief in society with regard to origins science, many Christians immediately resort to this belief rather than an axiom of biblical authority. In doing this, the society we are witnessing to sees us as being inconsistent and irrelevant. Many attempt to explain a non-literal Genesis by inputting human philosophy that is not in the text and yet accept a literal gospel without inputting human philosophy into the text.

Evolutionary and long-age thinking has done great damage to our culture and is now one of the great modern barriers to Christian thought and the delivery of the gospel. Our young people in a postmodern age are seeing the Bible as less and less authoritative, and sadly, in the main, the Church is not giving them answers to what truly are the greatest attacks on biblical authority. While this level of "intellectual" or "rational" skepticism was not necessarily a barrier to David Livingstone in Africa, the result of the thinking of David Livingstone's time is very apparent today. David Livingstone died in 1873, two years after Darwin wrote *The Descent of Man* (which was not widely distributed until around 1874), a book that was not particularly complimentary toward the people group Livingstone was witnessing to in that they were seen as being "less evolved." Yet his acceptance of long-age presuppositions rather than biblical authority would have given Livingstone little ammunition to deal with the problem of evolutionary thinking had its problems arrived on his mission field.

In 2006 America's Research Group (a major behavioral research organization) conducted a survey on the shift away from church attendance. Within this survey a common factor appeared: more people were questioning the authority of the Bible, particularly from high school age. A staggering 82 percent of people surveyed (about the underlying belief reasons they left the church) said that they did not believe because they doubt the accuracy and truth of the biblical account of history. Of these people, the majority claimed they doubted because of such issues as the age of the earth, Genesis disproved by science, alleged contradictions, errors written by men, and the death and suffering issue. When asked if there was one idea that they questioned more than any other, 86 percent claimed one of the following:[5]

> That there really was an Adam and Eve
> That there really was a Noah's Flood
> That the earth is young and not old
> That the days of creation were 24 hours each

A lack of defense in relation to these matters has not helped the Church in our mission for the gospel. So often we talk about the only need being to tell people the simple gospel of Christ, and this is true — but also not true. We must evangelize with a knowledge of our society, and we must do it in the spirit of being willing and able to defend that which we believe. I am sure that David Livingstone had no intention of compromising the gospel. Yet the same practice of merging human long-age philosophy with biblical teaching has presented a much bigger barrier to the gospel in today's culture given the general acceptance of evolutionary thinking and instruction in education facilities. Sadly, because many pastors have also

5. Ken Ham and Britt Beemer, *Already Gone* (Green Forest, AR: Master Books, 2009). America's Research Group, Ltd. is a full-service market and behavioral research firm offering expertise in all phases of survey research from questionnaire design to final report preparation.

been influenced by long-age philosophy, it also means that it is now more important than ever for dad and mom church attendees to be diligent and discerning in relation to what they are hearing from pulpits. Even in this book I have used a couple of good quotes from Christian brothers whom I could not endorse when it came to their teaching in Genesis. When I discuss authors and books with close friends I often use my "Genesis Disclaimer." My father used to say it this way: "The Bible is a great commentary on commentaries." In case of misunderstanding, I must emphasize that I am not suggesting that the only people who should communicate the gospel are those who have a consistent understanding of biblical authority in Genesis. I am, however, suggesting that we should all be consistent in our acceptance of biblical authority in the entirety of Scripture for two reasons: (1) it is God's Word, not ours, and His doctrine needs to be held in our closed hands; (2) contextualizing the gospel for our society means understanding that they do not believe we are answering their questions in relation to biblical relevance, authority, and, in particular, origins.

David Livingstone (a truly great hero of the faith) fell into the trap of allowing the influence of Roderick Murchison to impact his understanding of Genesis and therefore the age of the earth. He allowed the concept of neutrality to influence his interpretation of evidence. This is no different today in what has happened to the Christian Church but on a much wider scale. We now have solid statistics that reveal a large percentage of our culture is disengaged from the message of the gospel. This is due to the inability to accept biblical authority in the foundational area of Genesis. Disappointing as the statistics quoted above are, they are not a surprise.

If you are a pastor, lecturer, or Bible teacher of influence you will be under great pressure to maintain the most popular academic positions, and, sadly, they are not a straightforward reading of Genesis 1. To use a phrase borrowed from my pastor: "Even a dead dog can follow the current of the stream — it takes a live one to swim against it." Please consider for the sake of the gospel in our culture that we need "live dogs" more than ever, and you don't have to give up scientific credibility to be one. (Again see the reading material in the appendix.)

JEWS AND GREEKS

The Apostle Paul had a very different ministry to his apostolic peers. His initial ministry, while he himself was once considered a Jew of Jews, focused attention on the Gentiles. In his book *Why Won't They Listen?*, Ken Ham discussed the difference between the evangelistic style of Paul and that of Peter. Peter preached to Jews who knew and believed the foundations of the gospel from the Old Testament Scriptures. The Jews understood creation, the Fall, sin, and even their need for redemption through sacrifice. Paul, on the other hand, at Mars Hill was speaking to an audience of Greeks who had no foundational knowledge from Genesis. While we read of Peter simply talking about the gospel of Jesus with the Jews, we see Paul starting his gospel outreach to the Greeks from a very different point. Acts 17:23–31:

> Therefore, the One whom you worship without knowing, Him I proclaim to you: God, who made the world and everything in it, since He is Lord of heaven and earth, does not dwell in temples made with hands. Nor is He worshiped with men's hands, as though He needed anything, since He gives to all life, breath, and all things. And He has made from one blood every nation of men to dwell on all the face of the earth, and has determined their preappointed times and the boundaries of their dwellings, so that they should seek the Lord, in the hope that they might grope for Him and find Him, though He is not far from each one of us; for in Him we live and move and have our being, as also some of your own poets have said, "For we are also His offspring." Therefore, since we are the offspring of God, we ought not to think that the Divine Nature is like gold or

silver or stone, something shaped by art and man's devising. Truly, these times of ignorance God overlooked, but now commands all men everywhere to repent, because He has appointed a day on which He will judge the world in righteousness by the Man whom He has ordained. He has given assurance of this to all by raising Him from the dead.

Ken states:

The Greek culture was very complex with many different competing philosophies. While they saw "sin" and "evil" in their culture and recognized the importance of structure and laws, they had no concept of an absolute authority, absolute truth, or the inherent sin nature of man. The Greeks had no understanding concerning their first ancestor, Adam, and the concept of original sin — nor had they received the law of Moses. Therefore these people could not understand or accept the absolute authority of the Creator God, the lawgiver.[6]

He further says:

The Greeks listening to Paul on Mars Hill in Athens did not have the foundational knowledge to understand the gospel. . . . Trying to get the Greeks to understand the gospel would be like attempting to build a skyscraper on the foundation of a small family home. The Greek culture had the wrong foundation. If a builder wanted to construct a skyscraper, he would have to first of all remove the wrong foundation. Then he would need to build the right foundation before the rest of the structure could be started.[7]

We certainly live in a culture that is closer to the Greek culture than the Jewish. Our society is bombarded by competing

6. Ken Ham, *Why Won't They Listen?* (Green Forest, AR: Master Books, 2002), p. 52–53.
7. Ibid.

philosophies and has little if no understanding of the gospel foundations in creation and the Fall. As a result, we live in a culture that has no answers for such issues as death and suffering or our purpose in the world. We also have many people from within the Church telling us on a consistent basis to simply preach Christ and the Cross. The gospel message the modern Church is telling us we must preach is a Peter message. It's a good message and it's a correct message and God saves through it in an amazing way. If, however, we are to preach with understanding and relevance according to our culture, we must also be prepared to preach a Paul message and be willing to defend it via a Peter command: "But sanctify the Lord God in your hearts, and always be ready to give a defense to everyone who asks you a reason for the hope that is in you, with meekness and fear" (1 Pet. 3:15).

While thinking about this chapter, I noticed a song being played on our local Christian radio station in Brisbane. The song, by an artist named Sam Sparro, is called "Black and Gold." As I listened to the lyrics I wondered instantly why the song was being played on a Christian station. The first verse of the song talks about a time when fish came out of the water and walked on land, and when monkeys came down from the trees and started talking. It went on to say that if "You" (God) are not really there, we are all just matter and we may as well not be here. I came home and watched an interview on the Internet with Sam Sparro, who described his song as searching for some higher being, maybe God. The message we get is that evolution is now a presupposition in which our society views the world, and if we don't find God somehow we may as well not be here because evolution clearly teaches that we are nothing but matter. My point is that there are millions of Sam Sparros in the world who are looking for God. This song is representative of popular culture and became one of the highest-selling singles in Australia, the United States, and the United Kingdom for 2008.

We have a message to share with people who have been indoctrinated in a philosophy that makes no sense of the message we desire to deliver. Our message comes from a Book that the world sees as being full of errors, inconsistency, and irrelevance, and statistics show that they don't generally seem to be getting answers. This is the lostness of the world we live in. But we do have answers and we do have an omnipotent God. God's Word has provided amazing answers to make sense of this world and show the consistency and credibility of His gospel message. Let us also never forget that the Holy Spirit is the author of change in the heart of man and gives a recipient of the gospel ears to hear.

We have this amazing message to share with our community, not out of any selfish motive, but because of two vitally important reasons:

1. The Great Commission: our response to Christ in obedience

> And Jesus came and spoke to them, saying, "All authority has been given to Me in heaven and on earth. Go therefore and make disciples of all the nations, baptizing them in the name of the Father and of the Son and of the Holy Spirit, teaching them to observe all things that I have commanded you; and lo, I am with you always, even to the end of the age." Amen (Matt. 28:18–20).

Jesus Christ, our Lord and Savior, has given us a command: GO! MAKE DISCIPLES! This is not a suggestion or a preference but a command. It is the command that David Livingstone responded to and the command many missionaries for Christ have responded to. But it is also a command that every Christian must respond to. It is not a command just for Apostles, but for all who follow and worship Christ. Every Christian is called to be salt and light in the world, and every Christian is called to be Christ's witness. We are all called to be living and communicating the gospel, and we do so under the authority of Christ.

Just one verse prior to the Great Commission we see a profound art, "When they saw Him, they worshiped Him; but some doubted" (Matt. 28:17). Jesus appeared to the 11 Apostles, and while some initially doubted (for example, Thomas, who later proclaimed Him Lord and God), they *worshiped* Him. We need to consider the magnitude of this. They worshiped Christ as God, acknowledging that He is the omnipotent, omniscient, and omnipresent Creator and King of the universe. We often read the Bible and it seems so easy to separate it as simply an instructive word rather than realizing it is God's instructive Word. When we read Scripture it is the same as the Apostles hearing the words from the mouth of Jesus. It is almost impossible to get a sense of the atmosphere of the 11 standing in front of Jesus the risen Lord. If there was any doubt among them, Jesus then told them that *all authority* is His. If you are wondering who is giving you the command to go out and tell others of the message of Christ, it is Christ who is God in all authority. It is not just the gentle Christ who called the little children to come, it is not just the Christ who was the meek and lowly Lamb of sacrifice, but it is the great risen Lord and Lion of judgment. He is the Creator of the universe and the One who stands at the last day in victory.

The Great Commission is often overlooked as a mighty command of God. Christ does not *want* us to witness to our friends and family and neighbors, He *commands* it! In reverence to the great God of the universe, the 11 worshiped Him and then went out and witnessed literally to death.

For many years I ignored this command of God. He actually asks us to make disciples. For a long time it seemed that this command was not even on my radar, but I thank God that He made me feel more and more uncomfortable about the fact that I was not witnessing for Him. I had virtually no non-Christian friends, and while I worked in a non-Christian environment, my life and social scene were in the church. I don't know why this was the case, because I had seen my dad and mum constantly witnessing to people, but I suppose it is because like many human beings, I put myself before God. In 1993 a wonderful thing happened to me. Through a transfer of employment, God placed Trish and I and our brand-new daughter in a new community 15 hours' drive away from "home" (Brisbane). At Charters Towers in the far north of the state of Queensland we attended a small church where the pastor and many in the congregation were not interested in sitting idly by and ignoring the Great Commission. At least once each week my pastor would knock on my bedroom window and tell me to get out of bed and come and pray with him. (Yes, he actually did that.) Roy (my pastor) and Andrew, who would become one of my best friends, would pray for the town of Charters Towers, and then we would go around and knock on some doors with free copies of the Bible and ask to speak with people.

Door knocking is not something I have done for a long time now, but what a great way to give you some boldness. We had very poor success, but I realized something very important. God does not measure success in results but in obedience. I actually began communicating the gospel. We then created a tool to help us better do this in our home. We found that we needed to present the gospel like Paul, to Greeks who had been grounded in opposing philosophies. This tool has had such an impact for us and others that it has been published through Answers in Genesis and called "Answers for Life."[8] We praise God for opening our eyes to the wonderful command of the Great Commission.

Trish and I have seen a number of people come to know the Lord through being obedient to God's Great Commission. Two of them are our own children. Some people in this world have seen many more. But success to God is not about results but obedience. David Livingstone in his writings accounted for very few converts in Africa. But success to God is not about results but obedience, and David Livingstone's obedience opened the way for a flood of mission to that continent. My brother Ken has rarely had the opportunity to personally introduce someone to Christ. But success to God is not about results but obedience, and through his obedience

---

8. "Answers for Life" is a small group curriculum available from www.answersingenesis.org.

in preaching and teaching the credibility of the gospel, thousands of testimonies have flooded in to Answers in Genesis of people who have come to know Christ.

Christ has also commanded us to GO! While many churches have modeled evangelism on the basis of coming into the church as a central point, this is not what Christ has commanded. In a very clever way, many churches have adopted an approach that matches the needs of a consumer society. With great appeal to the community, the seeker-sensitive movement has learned how to market a church that meets the needs of a product-oriented community. Repentance and coming judgment for sin do not attract consumers. I often hear the advertisements for churches and church conferences attempting to be seeker sensitive on my local Christian radio station, and the emphasis is fiercely positive. "If you want a great life, we have the answer." Product and solution.

The biblical model is that we gather as God's people in fellowship around His Word for edification as the local body (1 Cor. 11–14). In obedience to the Great Commission we go out into the world for the sake of the gospel. This does not mean that the church shouldn't be contextual for the community around it. In fact, our churches should be preaching in order to equip the congregation for reaching out to the community around us. This would also be relevant to community members who come among us. Our churches should certainly be trying to use the communication tools of our day, and that means the use of good sound equipment, multimedia, the Internet, and other useful tools of our time. We should also be doing everything we can to welcome those who come among us. But we should commit our gatherings to the primary purpose of building strong believers based in the authoritative truth of God's Word and armed with the gospel armor to go into the world. This is the purpose of the Church and the command of the Great Commission.

There really is a burden in my heart to see churches more committed to equip members to meet the needs in our societies. Among other needs that the Church can minister to in order to witness Christ, there is a great need in our society to see the relevance of the authority of Scripture. We certainly do live in a society in which a large percentage have ignored Christ due to the indoctrination of worldly philosophies. My burden is for church leaders to help our congregations defend against the great attack that has been squarely aimed at the Book of Genesis to undermine the gospel. Real answers here would provide real relevance "out there."

To the readers of this book, I would suggest you follow three simple steps in obedience to the Great Commission in being relevant to the society we live in.

1. Pray for courage and wisdom.

2. Equip yourself with answers from God's Word and credible sources that align with the full authority of God's Word.

3. One person at a time, have real gospel conversations with your non-Christian family and friends. (If you don't have any, go out and make some — be hospitable.)

2. We are obligated by love and gratitude.

This is where we will end this book. It is in response to what we have from God.

When I think of what God has given me, I am truly overwhelmed. If I have nothing in this world, I have everything through Christ. To know that one day I am going to be in His presence for eternity makes me realize that nothing in this world is essential to me other than my relationship with Him.

Christians are people who truly understand that we are not deserving of the grace we have been given. We are those who rejected God as King in our life. We have looked upon ourselves as gods and worshiped our own desires. The great and terrible tragedy in this world is that we as humans shook our fists at the One who created us to be in His image and to reflect His glory. The judgment humanity faces is a just and holy outcome because we have rebelled against a righteous and perfect God.

Have you ever meditated on what you are deserving of and what you have been saved from? I don't think any of us can fathom the intensity of wrath from an omnipotent God. But on the positive side, I don't think any of us can fathom the glorious splendor of being called His children for all eternity and living in His pure shining glory.

The God who created us, who we sinned against, gave up all power and prestige to place Himself in poverty as a servant and be our once-and-for-all sacrifice. The wrath that we have no comprehension of in relation to its intensity has already been taken upon His shoulders. Charles Wesley said it best for all of us. *"And can it be that I should gain an interest in the Savior's blood? Died he for me who caused His pain, for me who Him to death pursued? Amazing love! How can it be that thou, my God, shouldst die for me?"*[9]

Paul certainly had this perspective as well. He would often compare his poverty as a human to the amazing wonder of Christ's grace: *"To me, who am less than the least of all the saints, this grace was given, that I should preach among the Gentiles the unsearchable riches of Christ"* (Eph. 3:8).

As I meditate on the amazing wonder of my own salvation I often get a sense of great and overwhelming gratitude. Not only that, but it can never be taken away from me. Romans 8 tells us that there is no power that can separate us from the love of God and that we who are in Christ Jesus, while guilty, are not condemned. The sense of pardon for a Christian is an overwhelming consideration. I challenge you to meditate on your pardon in Christ and consider that it is possible for you to have no desire to share that experience.

We are bound by love to share this gospel. We are bound by gratitude to share the truth of God's Word with a society blinded by the philosophies of this world. We are prepared in His grace to meet His command, but we do it from a sense of desiring to please Him.

---

9. "And Can It Be," http://www.cyberhymnal.org/htm/a/c/acanitbe.htm.

It is only with the authentic gospel work in our hearts through the power of the Holy Spirit that we can truly be filled with such gratitude. An easy-to-believe, seeker-sensitive, feel-good gospel does not bring the awe of God and the overwhelming sense of relief that we can only obtain from the authentic gospel preached from God's authoritative Word. We have already discussed that this gospel message is hard to believe, but there truly is only one authentic gospel and it is a gospel with great power and authority over our lives because it is God's. It is the gospel that brings true believers to their knees in overflowing gratitude to our Savior. Before ending this book we should again remind ourselves of the aspects that make this gospel both authoritative and authentic.

- Man has rejected his Creator for self-worship. This is sin. It has affected us all and we are in no way able to rectify our depraved nature on our own.

- God's judgment for sin is righteous and eternal, and every man and woman on earth is deserving of God's just punishment.

- Christ, who is God, came to earth in fullness of God and yet fullness of man. He came born of a virgin, was perfectly sinless, and gave Himself as the once-and-for-all sacrifice to take on the just wrath of God in our place on a Cross.

- Christ died and yet rose three days later in victory over sin and reigns eternally and will return in final judgment.

- We are saved by God's grace alone, through faith in Christ alone. Not by works so that any man could boast. Salvation is all of God. We are to repent and believe, and this as well is a gift of God.

Whenever I think of this wonderful gospel I see the authentic saving power of God, but I also see His great authority to redeem His lost and judge His scoffers. I am overwhelmed that I am one of His redeemed lost. I am compelled by gratitude to help others know His truth. I do not blindly believe in a timeless tale. I am convinced of the firmest of foundations that this message is supported by. The gospel is the doorway to everlasting life in perfect worship of our Creator, and it is hung on the frame of God's authoritative Word and hinged with the strongest of evidence. The world must know.

GOD'S FAME, NOT OURS

Evangelism is not about our own fame in this world but God's. In both the Great Commission of Matthew 28 and in the further commission of Acts 1:8, the job of the Church is to spread the news of Christ to the outermost parts of the earth.

If God is truly the authority, it is His name that should be the foremost name on the lips of this planet. God has always shown His glory and fame to the nations of this world. When many of the God-hating nations desiring their own glory were out to destroy Israel, it was God's fame through Israel whereby these nations witnessed His authority. The Apostles were persecuted by this world and all except John ended up as martyrs, and yet through their mission of the gospel, God's fame has spread in reviving glory in the lives of men and women through the ages.

This world needs to know that our God is Creator, Judge, Savior, and Lord. His ways are just and His word is final. His authority is self-attesting and all-encompassing. He is the great God of the universe for all eternity. The spread of this fame in the lives of men and women is our Great Commission. We complete our missionary task with motivation to see Him famously glorified as the authoritative God of all.

Now to Him who is able to keep you from stumbling, and to present you faultless before the presence of His glory with exceeding joy, to God our Savior, who alone is wise, be glory and majesty, dominion and power, both now and forever. Amen (Jude 1:24–25).

When it comes to the delivery of the gospel to a society looking for relevance: authority matters.

CLOSING COMMENTS

Together we have journeyed through the substance of authority. We have come to see something of the wonder of the originator of authority (God). And we have considered some aspects of Christian living in which God's authority must reign if we are to be His true worshipers.

It is entirely appropriate that we have finished this book with some thoughts on the mission of the gospel. It is God's authority that makes this message what it is. This is the only message in the world that can make us wise to salvation and lead us to an everlasting relationship with our Savior and Lord. If this message does not come from the ultimate in authority, we are kidding ourselves by believing it. The Bible authentically shows, however, that it does. Strong hinges.

I encourage you to ask yourself one real and very personal question. This is a question you may ask in relation to your own life, the way you read the Bible, the way you do church, the way you view worship, the way you view the world, or the way you commit to the mission of the gospel . . . and so on.

Who in practical reality is the authority: you or God?

Appendix

Confirming the Confirmable

There really was a worldwide flood, just look at the stony curse. Billions of dead things, buried in rock layers, laid down by water, all over the earth.[1] *— Ken Ham/Buddy Davis*

When science and the Bible differ, science has obviously misinterpreted its data.[2] *— Henry Morris*

I believe Jesus Christ was born of a virgin, rose from the dead, reigns in heaven, and is coming back in both glory and judgment on the great day to come. I believe this because my axiom is biblical authority; I need no other proof. What I would at least expect, however, is that God's Word would be an authentically accurate record. I would expect to read God's Word and where it relates to this world, I would expect to find that God's Word makes accurate sense of the world around me. I thank God that His Word allows me to confirm the confirmable.

1. From the lyrics to the song on this CD: www.answersingenesis.org/Public-Store/product/Buddy-Davis-The-Best-of-Buddy-Davis,5031,233.aspx.
2. http://en.wikiquote.org/wiki/Henry_M._Morris.

The idea of this appendix is to give a brief overview of some of the things in this world that show great confirmation of the Bible's history when we look at the evidence through the lens of biblical authority. We will not be able, and it is not my intention, to do anything other than scratch the surface and perhaps induce some curiosity in these matters. This is why at the end of this chapter I will provide a reading list. I would encourage you to take the time to understand the confirmable history of God's Word because it is directly linked to the questions being asked in our time. The Apostle Peter has told us to always be ready to give an answer for the hope that we have. Without being able to answer, I might never have had the true opportunity to share the grace of Jesus with my friend Ken, whose story I shared in chapter 8. We are powerless to give these answers without a strong stance on biblical authority. You could say that to be able to answer the most culturally relevant questions that our world is asking today, biblical authority matters and it matters a great deal. Let's look at a few examples through the lens of biblical authority.

DNA and Information

> In the beginning was the Word, and the Word was with God, and the Word was God (John 1:1).

When explaining the information in DNA, Dr. Jason Lisle comments in *The Ultimate Proof of Creation*:

> DNA also contains information. DNA (deoxyribonucleic acid) is a long molecule found within living cells and resembles a twisted ladder. The rungs of the ladder form a pattern of base pair triplets that represent amino acid sequences — the building blocks of proteins. DNA contains the "instructions" to build the organism. So, different organisms have different DNA patterns. DNA qualifies under the definition of information: it contains an encoded message (the base pair triplets represent amino acids) and

has an expected action (the formation of proteins) and an intended purpose (life).

Whenever we find any sort of information, certain rules or "theorems" apply. Here are two such theorems:

1. There is no known law of nature, no known process, and no known sequence of events that can cause information to originate by itself in matter.

2. When its progress along the chain of transmission events is traced backwards, every piece of information leads to a mental source, the mind of the sender.[3]

What Dr. Lisle is saying is that DNA is like a language, a language that has information that means something. The language has purpose and meaning and is intelligible. There is no source of logical information in the world that does not have at its source a mental wellspring. One cannot design a language unless one is able to communicate with meaning. Like DNA, a language has many variations of code (like letters) that form into words, sentences, and phrases. While some of my friends would debate it, this entire book is coming from a source of intelligence.

Looking at the wonderful language of DNA through biblical authority we can be amazed but not surprised that the information in DNA is complex and meaningful. My DNA is a major factor in determining why I am who I am, from my skin tone to my eye color, my height, the shape of my nose, and the length of my ear lobes. My DNA is a Steve Ham book. My DNA also represents where I came from and links me to both my mother and father. It is so overwhelmingly evident that DNA did not just appear. The two rules that Jason Lisle has stated (originally from Dr. Werner Gitt[4]) are indisputable. They are factual statements. All information has

---

3. Jason Lisle, *The Ultimate Proof of Creation* (Green Forest, AR: Master Books, 2009), p. 18–19.
4. Werner Gitt, *In the Beginning Was Information* (Green Forest, AR: Master Books, 2006), p. 70, 107.

an intelligent mind source. Yes, DNA is amazing, but we shouldn't be surprised when we read that the Bible attributes all life and all creation to God. He is the self-existent, eternal God with all power, knowledge, and presence. In the beginning was the Word, Jesus. He is our Creator God who by the very word of His mouth created the heavens and the earth and everything within. By His omniscient Word the code of our very being was written, and today we are still discovering more about that wonderful code that is so complex and so detailed in every respect. Even though sin has somewhat corrupted our DNA and today we experience deformities and hereditary illness, we can still, even today, see the wonder of God in the information in DNA.

BIOLOGY

As we read through Genesis 1 we see a specific and consistent creation ordinance. God created each living thing according to its kind (likely family or order level in the common classification scheme for most organisms). This relates to all living things. Basically we can say that all life on earth is created after its own kind by a simple and literal reading of Genesis 1.

Looking through biblical glasses, this is exactly what we see. Dogs come from dogs, pelicans come from pelicans, dolphins come from dolphins, and we could go on all day considering all of the plant, animal, bird, and marine life on the planet. This concept is in direct opposition to molecules to man evolution that evolutionary scientists believe — that in the past animals have slowly changed over time to evolve into something entirely different.

In the last point we discussed something in relation to DNA and the wonder of information that is contained in our DNA. For us to accept an evolutionary presupposition when looking at biological kinds, we have to accept that DNA can change over time to include by chance, random processes the addition of new information. As an example, this would mean that by chance it is possible for a reptile to have a random addition of new information to produce something that it is not already programmed for — perhaps feathers. On the basis of operational science (testable, repeatable, falsifiable, and observable in the present), the consideration of a lizard developing feathers is obscure to say the least. Yet this is precisely what evolutionists would have us believe as a presupposition about the past in relation to their idea. We would have to accept that random chance could actually add new information in DNA to produce one kind of animal from a completely different kind of animal over time.

One of the main arguments an evolutionist will use to entice us to consider their idea is natural selection. In fact, most evolutionists have taught natural selection as a major mechanism for molecules to man evolution. An evolutionist would consider natural selection to be a process whereby organisms best fit for their environment will survive and pass along these traits, resulting in the fittest surviving and perpetuating the trait in a progressive manner through time. Over millions of years, this process allows one kind of organism to evolve into another kind (e.g., dinosaurs into birds). Natural selection has widely been taught as a major mechanism behind molecules to man evolution. Looking at natural selection with biblical glasses, however, a Christian should see it in an entirely different light. As a Christian, molecular biologist Dr. Georgia Purdom points out:

> From a creationist perspective, natural selection is a process whereby organisms possessing specific characteristics (reflective of their genetic make-up) survive better than others in a given environment or under a given selective pressure (i.e., antibiotic resistance in bacteria). Those with certain characteristics live, and those without them diminish in number or die. The problem for evolutionists is that natural selection is nondirectional — should the environment change or the selective pressure be removed, those organisms with previously selected characteristics are typically less able to deal with the changes and may be selected

against because their genetic information has decreased. Evolution of the molecules to man variety requires directional change. Thus, the term "evolution" cannot be rightly used in the context of describing what natural selection can accomplish.[5]

When Dr. Purdom looks at natural selection through her biblical authority lens she sees two main things.

First, the Bible tells us that kinds were created after their kind. Operational science shows natural selection to be a legitimate process. However, in reference to biblical authority we obtain another wonderful fact by looking at natural selection. Through our biblical lens we can see that it is evident that God designed and created organisms with a great amount of genetic diversity that could be selected for or against, resulting in certain characteristics depending on the circumstances. We see amazing diversity within each kind of organism as we look at our world today. Even simply considering dogs and all the different types of wild and domestic dogs, we see amazing variation. But what we see are dogs.

The second thing is that we should therefore expect that we would not be able to see new information within DNA actually increasing (e.g., the reptile/feathers example). We may see speciation and variation within a kind, but we will never see genetic change outside of those God-ordained design boundaries. Out of all the dogs in a cold climate, only those with long hair will likely survive or remain in that climate, thus eventually breeding out the genetic information for short hair. Our evolutionist friends may consider this to be "survival of the fittest" and a mechanism that would result in molecules to man evolution over time, when in fact it has simply been a decrease in genetic information bred out through environmental change (natural selection). At the end of the day, they are still dogs and information for short hair could only be reintroduced by again breeding with short-haired dogs. This too would not be an

5. Ken Ham, editor, *The New Answers Book 1* (Green Forest, AR: Master Books 2006), p. 272–273.

increase in information but only a reintroduction of the information that is already within the kind.

When I see variation within kinds I praise God for what I see. Within a kind there is displayed a God of order and design, and in variation in that kind we see a God of great wonder, creativity, and diversity. When we look at this world through the axiom of biblical authority, God's Word comes alive and gives us great cause to praise His awesome power and majesty. His special revelation makes perfect sense of the general revelation, and I bow my knees to His Kingship.

ASTRONOMY

There is something that I specifically love about astronomy through a biblical lens. It brings out the glory of God and the foolishness of man in such a clear way. Advances in technology have allowed us to travel into space and look back at our earth. We have satellites, spaceships, and even space stations and powerful radio telescopes reaching distances beyond our solar system and galaxy and the plethora of galaxies in the universe. In fact, even with what we can see today, there is still the distinct impression that we are only just scratching the surface of our amazing universe. The bottom line is that through technology we can now see what our forefathers never dreamed of, and it has shed enormous light on some of the theories of their day about our planet and the universe. Our modern technology has also left Scripture shining in brilliant wisdom. If only some of our forefathers had read the Bible more carefully and accepted God's authority more readily.

It is He who sits above the circle of the earth, and its inhabitants are like grasshoppers (Isa. 40:22).

He drew a circular horizon on the face of the waters (Job 26:10).

I consistently hear people calling Christians "flat earthers" and continuing to bring this up as a reason not to accept the authority of the Bible. They use the argument that we are "flat earthers" because we apparently reject science for Bible fables. Yet, imagine if the Church in the time when a flat earth was truly being promoted actually did stand on biblical authority. God's Word clearly indicates that the world is round. An axiom of biblical authority would have had the Church welcoming a spherical earth. Do we need to go further today on commenting on the sphere of our planet? Go out and buy a globe and remind yourself each time you look at it that biblical authority towers over human reason that is not based on God's Word (even when that reason is perpetuated within the Church).

> He stretches out the north over empty space; He hangs the earth on nothing (Job 26:7).

While it would have been very difficult for the author of Job to understand this, today with satellite photos of our earth we see that indeed we are floating on nothing.

> Who stretches out the heavens like a curtain and spreads them out like a tent to dwell in (Isa. 40:22).

From *Taking Back Astronomy*, Dr. Jason Lisle, PhD:

> The Bible indicates in several places that the universe has been "stretched out" or expanded. . . . This would suggest that the universe has actually increased in size since its creation. God has stretched it out. He has expanded it (and is perhaps still expanding it). This verse must have seemed very strange when it was first written. The universe certainly doesn't look as if it is expanding. After all, if you look at the night sky tonight, it will appear about the same size as it did the previous night, and the night before that. Ancient star maps appear virtually identical to the night sky today. Could the universe really have been expanded? It must have been hard to believe at the time.

In fact secular scientists once believed that the universe was eternal and unchanging. The idea of an expanding universe would have been considered nonsense to most scientists of the past. It must have been tempting for Christians to reject what the Bible teaches about the expansion of the universe. Perhaps some Christians tried to "reinterpret" Isaiah 40:22, and read it in an unnatural way so that they wouldn't have to believe in an expanding universe. When the world believes one thing and the Bible teaches another, it is always tempting to think God got the details wrong, but God is never wrong.[6]

These are just three of many truths the Bible gives us about God's creation. While men without the technology of such items as telescopes previously had no way of looking into many of these truths until very recently, the Bible has had the truth of the universe within its pages for thousands of years.

It is therefore extraordinary that human arrogance has brought us to assumptions about the beginning of our universe that totally defy the authority of God's Word. Most people, for example, who believe in billions of years believe in the "big bang." The big bang is a secular model of the origin of the universe that proposes that all mass, energy, and space were contained in a point that rapidly expanded to become stars and galaxies over billions of years.

What does the Bible tell us about the big bang? Well, as Christians we can have one very big problem with it. The Bible tells us that the sun and stars were not created until day 4 of creation, yet the big-bang theory attempts to explain the origin of the entire universe of both terrestrial and celestial bodies in one event billions of years ago. This simply does not correlate with Scripture and purposes to explain an origin in a naturalistic way without a creator. Just like the Bible has shed light on the ignorance of the human theory of a flat earth, the Bible also sheds light on the big bang. The

6. Jason Lisle, *Taking Back Astronomy* (Green Forest, AR: Master Books, 2006), p. 28–29.

biggest light will be shed on the day of consummation when Christ will eternally make all things right. There will be new heavens and earth, and those in Christ will reign with Him eternally. The belief in a big bang proposes that the universe will gradually die a "heat death." One day there will not be a single person that will deny the authority of the Bible, but sadly for many it will be too late.

We could continue considering so many more confirmable truths of the Bible as it relates to science. Geology in particular has an incredible source of biblical-confirming evidence as we see the visible destruction of the Genesis 6 Flood in the records of the fossil layers. We could consider anthropology and the world's people groups as they confirm the account of the Tower of Babel in Genesis 11 where God disbursed people according to language differences and thus isolated gene pools. This is where I refer you to the reading list and ask that you continue to equip yourselves to confirm the confirmable.

Before we end this chapter, however, I cannot move forward without talking about some of the confirmable evidence about the Scriptures themselves.

THE BIBLE AND PROPHECY — THE DEAD SEA SCROLLS

The Dead Sea Scrolls were found in 1947. A shepherd boy named Muhammad stumbled across the scrolls (there were over 40,000 inscribed fragments) whilst searching for a lost goat. Archaeologists have dated the scrolls to more than a century before Christ's birth. This not only shows that the Old Testament was written before the time of Christ, but it also qualified how accurate the copyists were, as there are very few discrepancies between these documents and the existing documents (the oldest documents we had before this find were written around A.D. 900, hence very few discrepancies over a 1,000-year period.[7]

---

7. Steve Ham and Terry Cave, *Answers for Life*, leaders guide (Hebron, KY: Answers in Genesis, 2008), p. 46..

None of the very few copying discrepancies had any bearing on the message of the Old Testament Scriptures. God's Word in itself has stood the test of time. The Old Testament was written between 1500 B.C. and 400 B.C. and contains over 60 prophecies about Jesus, written by various authors (inspired by the Holy Spirit) who lived hundreds of years apart and foretold varied specific details about Jesus and what He would do. This is an outstanding fact of the Bible. The Dead Sea Scrolls confirm the authenticity of the Old Testament, but it is the message of the Old Testament that is truly outstanding. From the very first book, God's Word has pointed to Jesus Christ. The prophecies in the Old Testament are a wonderful authenticity of God's authority over the entire past, present, and future of this world. Let's consider just a few.

The virgin birth:
> Therefore the Lord Himself will give you a sign: Behold, the virgin shall conceive and bear a Son, and shall call His name Immanuel (Isa. 7:14).

The Savior will come from Bethlehem:
> But you, Bethlehem Ephrathah, though you are little among the thousands of Judah, yet out of you shall come forth to Me the One to be Ruler in Israel, whose goings forth are from old, from everlasting (Mic. 5:2).

Jesus will be preceded by one preparing the way (John the Baptist):
> The voice of one crying in the wilderness: Prepare the way of the LORD; make straight in the desert a highway for our God (Isa. 40:3).

Jesus will perform miracles:
> Then the eyes of the blind shall be opened, and the ears of the deaf shall be unstopped. Then the lame shall leap like a deer, and the tongue of the dumb sing. For waters shall burst forth in the wilderness, and streams in the desert (Isa. 35:5–6).

Jesus' hands and feet would be pierced:
> For dogs have surrounded Me; the congregation of the wicked has enclosed Me. They pierced My hands and My feet (Ps. 22:16).

Actually many prophecies of Jesus would be fulfilled on the one day of His crucifixion. The Old Testament has prophesies about being betrayed by a friend (Ps. 41:9), being betrayed for 30 pieces of silver (Zech. 11:12), His garments being divided and lots cast (Ps. 22:18), about being given vinegar on the Cross (Ps. 69:21), His bones not being broken (Ps. 34:20), His side being pierced (Zech. 12:10), darkness falling over the land (Amos 8:9), and being buried in a rich man's tomb (Isa. 53:9).

Whether it is archaeology, geology, biology, anthropology, astronomy, information science, history, or prophecy, the Bible is God's authoritative Word confirmed by the evidence and logic applied to its pages. The Bible is NOT just the authority in matters of faith and conduct but in every matter that it speaks about, and God is the authority over all. God in His great grace has given us the ability to confirm the confirmable in His revelation to all mankind. But this should never be our goal in itself. The Bible is the great message of Jesus Christ, our need for Him as our Savior, His great atoning work on the Cross to take God's wrath for our sin on His shoulders, His conquering of sin and death in the Resurrection, His equipping of the Church to spread His glorious news, and His ultimate return when He will again put right all things to the glory and eternal honor of God.

We have previously explored how difficult the gospel is to accept. Only on the highest of authorities can we accept this gospel that requires us to acknowledge that we are evil in the sight of God and are subject to His great wrath. It is also the gospel that requires us to believe in a virgin birth, the incarnation of God, the Son of God being sentenced to the vilest of deaths, and that He rose from the dead and ascended into heaven after showing Himself to His followers. This gospel also requires us to deny ourselves, repent, and accept Christ. In the main, the world finds this message unacceptable, and man's beliefs (especially evolution) have been very effective in spreading the evil one's message that the Bible containing this gospel is unreliable.

The world is looking for answers to their criticisms and beliefs. They are asking why science and the Bible don't correlate, why there is death and suffering, and why the Bible is relevant. We must be equipped to answer the world's questions, and as Christians we must be ready to stand on the authority of Scripture and look through the biblical lens at this world to provide real and relevant answers that are authentic and authoritative. They are not authoritative because they are our answers, but because we can answer on the only authority worth claiming — the Lord our God.

Confirming the confirmable is one of the most amazing evangelistic tools that the Church has (and has always had). The Lord Jesus confirmed His own authority while on earth by healing the sick, making the blind to see and the lame to walk, raising the dead, and casting out demons — and He did this in front of many crowds of people. If Jesus had not done any of that it would not have reduced His authority in any way, but for our sakes Jesus authenticated His authority among us. He then displayed this wonderful power through sending the Holy Spirit, and the Apostles also showed the signs and wonders of Christ as the Church saw the endorsement of the Apostles as Christ's chosen leaders in establishing His Church. Through this apostolic authority, the Lord Jesus has given us the gospels and the epistles as His authoritative word among us today. It is His self-authenticating word with a confirmable history.

While God's authority needs no proving, confirmation of His authority has always been among us like a gracious gift allowing our fallible nature to come to terms with His authoritative power. God has displayed and confirmed His authority through all the ages to allow men to turn back to Him and deny their own kingship for His ultimate Kingship. The world has attacked biblical authority with a ferocious intensity, and what is worse, the attack has even come from within the Church. Sometimes the attack comes from a blatant opposition and sometimes from a vague neutrality, but we must realize that anything other than an acceptance of God's unrivaled authority is a form of idolatry placing mankind in authority over God. Please allow me to staunchly and dogmatically say that both denial and neutrality are unacceptable to God.

It is therefore time to ask yourself again: how firm are your hinges? Are the hinges to the door of your faith tightly screwed into a solid frame of biblical authority? And when your friends ask, are you able to answer their questions with the gracious and overwhelming confirmations that the Lord has given us?

Authority matters — it matters a great deal. (And it's confirmable!)

READING LIST

Answers Magazine, from Answers in Genesis.

Answers for Life, apologetics small group study, Steve Ham and Terry Cave, Answers in Genesis. 2008.

www.answersingenesis.org.

Darwin's Plantation, Ken Ham and Charles Ware (Green Forest, AR: Master Books, 2007).

How Could a Loving God? Ken Ham (Green Forest, AR: Master Books, 2007).

In the Beginning Was Information, Werner Gitt (Green Forest, AR: Master Books, 2006).

The Lie: Evolution, Ken Ham (Green Forest, AR: Master Books, 1987).

More than a Carpenter, Josh McDowell (Wheaton, IL: Tyndale House Publ. 1977).

The New Answers Book 1, Ken Ham, editor (Green Forest, AR: Master Books, 2006).

The New Answers Book 2, Ken Ham, editor (Green Forest, AR: Master Books, 2008).

The New Answers Book 3, Ken Ham, editor (Green Forest, AR: Master Books, 2010).

New Evidence that Demands a Verdict, Josh McDowell (Nashville, TN: Thomas Nelson, 1999).

Nothing but the Truth, Brian Edwards (Darlington, UK: Evangelical Press, 2006).

Taking Back Astronomy, Jason Lisle (Green Forest, AR: Master Books, 2009).

The Ultimate Proof of Creation, Jason Lisle (Green Forest, AR: Master Books, 2009).

Why 27? Brian Edwards (Darlington, UK: Evangelical Press).

Raising Godly Children in an Ungodly World

Ken Ham and Steve Ham

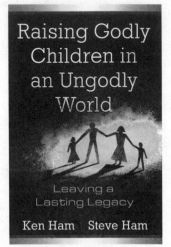

Christian families are struggling in a culture hostile to Christian values, and increasingly find themselves searching for answers and strategies to be more effective. Parents also face a disturbing trend of young people leaving home and leaving the Church — and want to ensure their children have a strong foundation of biblical faith and understanding. Discover how to create an incredible faith legacy in your family! *Raising Godly Children in an Ungodly World* presents empowering insight for:

• Surviving the culture wars as a family
• Educating children — the Bible offers guidance
• Practical tips for raising spiritually healthy children
• Solutions to the root cause of dysfunctional families
• Discovering biblical authority as a parent
• Discipline — necessary and lovingly administered

Ken Ham is joined by his brother, Steve Ham, in presenting this powerful look at how the principles and truth of Genesis are vital to the strong and lasting foundation of a family. Sharing their own stories of growing up in a "Genesis" family and sharing this legacy within their own families, it is an intensely personal and practical guide for parents.

paperback • 240 pages • $12.99
ISBN-13: 978-0-89051-542-6
ISBN-10: 0-89051-542-5

Available at Christian bookstores nationwide